The CONVEX STRIKE

It will transform the Game

The Convex Swing delivers "Frictionless" Distance by Design

CHEONG Sai Fah

In collaboration with YT Siew

INDIA • SINGAPORE • MALAYSIA

Copyright © Cheong Sai Fah 2025
All Rights Reserved.

ISBN 979-8-89277-276-1

This book has been published with all efforts taken to make the material error-free after the consent of the author. However, the author and the publisher do not assume and hereby disclaim any liability to any party for any loss, damage, or disruption caused by errors or omissions, whether such errors or omissions result from negligence, accident, or any other cause.

While every effort has been made to avoid any mistake or omission, this publication is being sold on the condition and understanding that neither the author nor the publishers or printers would be liable in any manner to any person by reason of any mistake or omission in this publication or for any action taken or omitted to be taken or advice rendered or accepted on the basis of this work. For any defect in printing or binding the publishers will be liable only to replace the defective copy by another copy of this work then available.

A Convex Strike using a Driver

Backswing

Downswing

Rotational Follow-through*

* This imitates the distance-enhancing move of field sports like shot put. The right leg crosses over the left. (In Ben Hogan's swing, dragging the right foot at the finish limits its distance.)

The swing *pivots* on the left heel with its sole fan-sliding *off the ground*, a distance-enhancer.

Dedication

To my granddaughters, Avril Cheong Li-Yen and Ashley Cheong Zi Yen, who have given so much joy to those who have loved them so.

To The Royal Selangor Golf Club (Kuala Lumpur, Malaysia), for the joyous memories of half a century of golf with friends and family that have made my life more meaningful.

To my wife, Lim Yew Lan, who loves me enough to allow me to be the person that I am comfortable with.

To my son, Jack Cheong Tse Chiew, for living with his aging parents and doing things that make their lives more pleasant.

To my daughter, Cheong Ee-Laine, and my son-in-law, Zachary Hoffberg, for being thoughtful in many ways while abroad and on their regular home visits.

TABLE OF CONTENTS

AUTHOR

Sai Fah is the author of *The Reflex Convex Swing*.

He worked as a researcher focusing on improving the efficiency of processes pertaining to commodities such as natural rubber, oil palm, and cocoa.

He used a cause and effect analysis of existing processes that provided insights for improvement.

The same approach highlighted the deficiencies of the Ben Hogan Modern Swing. There were three major stumbling blocks that needed to be removed for the golf swing technique to progress.

He devised a new swing system that removed those stumbling blocks and also improved the mechanical efficiency of the golf swing.

The new, efficient Convex Swing System was able to execute the Convex Strike on the golf ball—a feat that has not been done before!

ACKNOWLEDGMENTS

To Alex Goh of Melbourne, Australia, who took the initial steps on this journey to make this book possible. Alex contacted me and asked me to coach him to acquire the Reflex Convex Swing. In about six months of intermittent lessons, he was able to acquire the reflex convex swing. He provided proof of concept that the Convex Swing is easy to learn and functional. That allowed me to use his swing sequence to post a coaching video on YouTube. Unfortunately, he was not able to devote more time to taking the swing to its ultimate destination, a Convex Strike.

To SIEW Yit Toong, better known as YT Siew, who took up the daunting challenge of acquiring the skills to perform the Convex Strike on the ball. In the process, he had to remodel his swing to the precepts of the reflex convex swing. Because he was a diligent worker with a very receptive mind, it didn't take him long to acquire the basic Convex Swing.

What took a long time was getting that extra strength in his left shoulder to push the left arm to the top of the backswing reliably and also in the rotational speed of the lower body required to do the Convex Strike on the ball. And the many refinements that made his swing more efficient and allowed him to perform the elusive Convex Strike reliably.

The last mile in his epic journey to do the Convex Strike required dedication and determination. YT overcame many obstacles along the way. To him, it is not whether but how to achieve the elusive Convex Strike. Without his persistence, belief, and effort, this Convex Strike on the golf ball—the Grail of Golf—would have remained a dream longer than necessary for the golfing community.

In the process, several concepts were stretched to their practical limits. In that respect, I would not have found a more compliant and determined collaborator for this project. I am truly indebted to him for making this dream of mine (and his too) a reality. Without his dogged determination to see this project through, this book may not have been published.

Through this arduous journey, he acquired in-depth and insightful knowledge about the golf swing. This will prepare him well to introduce the Convex Swing System to a wider audience. And perhaps find a world beater or two to establish the Convex Swing System in the future.

To my goddaughter, Audrey Ho Mei Lian, for being the first to use and play the pivot fan-slide movement. I used a photo collage of her swing to help my early students visualize and understand how it can be done. She also helped me compose and illustrate my coaching on YouTube. Her advice about the need to better distinguish the difference between the Convex Swing and the Convex Strike and the contents of the blurb prompted me to make my text more lucid.

To my son, Jack Cheong Tse Chiew, who took photos of me posing with the many elements of the Convex Swing. Those photos formed the basis of some illustrations that appear in this book. He helped me with the computer skills to write my books.

To my wife, Lim Yew Lan, who was patient enough to bear the many conversations that I had with YT while interrupting her enjoyment of K-movies, China-theme documentaries, and news. Her encouragement helped me persevere with my Convex Strike project.

01

THE CONVEX STRIKE: DISTANCE BY DESIGN

Distance is "The Holy Grail of Golf." [1]

Michael Haywood, the PGA Director of Golf Operations at Tucson Country Club in Arizona, made that claim at the 15th PGA Teaching & Coaching Summit (2017). The Summit focused on all manner of coaching tips and gadgets to gain extra distance.

The pursuit of distance has been relentless since Ben Hogan introduced the Modern Swing in 1957 in his book *Five Lessons: The Modern Fundamentals of Golf*. Hogan's swing has been the gold standard for half a century.

However, driving distance has only increased a meager 5% in the last two decades[2] (Bryson DeChambeau's 321.7 yards in 2021 compared to John Daly's 306.7 in 2001). This progress is glacial, given the advances in golf equipment and ball technology, suggesting that Hogan's swing has reached its technical limits.

This points to a long overdue need for a breakthrough in golf swing technique.

Most professional golfers have used the same basic Hogan Swing concepts. A common characteristic of the Hogan Swing is that the club shaft assumes a convex bend early in the downswing. Then, the shaft straightens and transitions to a concave bend before striking the ball.

They all strike the ball with a concave bend shaft, regardless of their strength or swing speed.

By contrast, the convex bend of an implement is known to be the stronger bend. The fishing rod uses the convex bend to cast the line and sinker. In pole vaulting (https://youtu.be/Fr_ksZ0PYm8, at time 1:25), the convex bend of the pole propels the athlete over the bar. The convex bend of the bow is also utilized in archery.

Conspicuously, the convex bend shaft has not been used to strike the golf ball.

Occasionally, the convex bend of the shaft has been speculated as a potentially more powerful way to strike the ball, but that idea remained dormant.

Why is this so?

Because a swing system had yet to be devised to deploy the convex bend of the shaft to strike the ball.

But that changed recently.

In 2020, *The Reflex Convex Swing* by CHEONG Sai Fah postulated that the new Convex Swing System can strike the golf ball with a convex bend shaft.

The Convex Swing System was devised to redress Hogan Swing's limitations. It built on some ideas propagated in Mindy Blake's *The Golf Swing of the Future*. The Convex Swing is a natural progression from some of Blake's ideas taken to their logical conclusion.

The Convex Swing System also incorporated many ideas prevalent in field sports to improve the mechanical efficiency of the golf swing.

It made the rotational movement of the lower body—a prevalent and dominant feature in field sports—the principal source of power in a golf swing.

It also reimagined the golf swing as an efficient system to generate energy during the backswing to deliver power in the downswing, propelling the ball further.

Guided by a focus on distance, a coherent swing system emerged with the potential to strike the ball in a revolutionary way — with a convex bend shaft.

The Three Foundational Core Principles of the Convex Swing

The Reflex Convex Swing introduces three core principles designed for distance. This swing system allows for the first time the probability of a convex bend shaft striking the ball.

The three core principles are:

1. The narrow 'armpit-width' stance[3] promotes rotational movement of the lower body while remaining wide enough to maintain stability (Figure 1.1). It is significantly narrower than the Hogan Swing 'shoulder-width' stance.

2. Both feet at the address are pre-turned radically *anti-clockwise* toward the target, the right foot 20 - 45 degrees, and the left 60 - 90 degrees[4] (Figure 1.1). This is to facilitate the *anti-clockwise* movement of the downswing.

3. The *anti-clockwise* rotational movement of the lower body is the prime motive source to power the downswing. This

import from field sports blends seamlessly with the narrow stance and the anti-clockwise orientation of both feet.

The Convex Swing System also introduces a novel 'frictionless' movement - the left foot pivot fan-slide[5] - to facilitate momentum throughout the downswing and impact zone.

These three core principles mutually reinforce each other to produce a powerful downswing force.

The pivot fan-slide is part of a unique quadruple trade-on system, resulting in a final effect greater than the sum of their individual parts.

The three core principles trade on each other to build momentum throughout the downswing, making the Convex Strike on the ball a reality.

Distance-Enhancing Features of the Key Elements

The Pre-turned Right Foot. The pre-turned right foot restricts hip turn, making it easier to generate maximum energy with a compact backswing. The body weight shifts toward the right hip/side with less movement of the left shoulder. The shoulder plane needs to rotate less around the swing axis.

The desired 60-degree[6] difference between the shoulder and hip plane, termed the X-Factor, is obtained early with a short, compact backswing, generating maximum potential energy to power the downswing.

The pre-turned right foot is also better positioned to initiate the *anti-clockwise* rotational movement of the lower body with an aggressive push off the ball of the right foot instead of the instep.

(This imitates the aggressive push off the ball of the right foot on the starting blocks of sprint events in athletics.)

The aggressive push off the ball of the right foot initiates the rotational movement of the lower body to transfer body weight to the left side, leg, and heel. This initial move down and the rotational movement of the lower body stretch the X-Factor further to generate more stored energy in the backswing.[6]

Rotation over a Narrow Stance: The lower body rotates more efficiently and stably over a narrow stance. The body weight and swing axis remain within the confines of the outer heels. (In field sports such as the hammer throw, shot put, and discus, the final throw is delivered over a narrow stance. So, the golf swing does not need to be any different.)

The Pre-turned Very Open Left Foot: The open left foot at the address points the hip plane left of the target; the resultant stretch felt in the left leg muscles at the top of the backswing helps trigger the push off the ball of the right foot in the first move down. This contributes to achieving the X-Factor Stretch.[6]

The open left foot facilitates the *anti-clockwise* downswing movement. It encourages body weight to be shifted onto the left heel. The rotational movement pivots on the left heel (and not on the ball or side) of the foot. The resultant left heel 'frictionless' pivot fan-slide movement, deployed throughout the impact zone, improves the rotational efficiency of the golf swing.

The pivot fan-slide allows the whole body to rotate around the swing axis on the left heel; the right leg revolves around the left leg and lands the right foot across the target line, allowing the momentum of the downswing to continue uninterrupted to a full finish. (For convenience, the revolving movement of the right leg around the left leg will be referred to as 'rotational follow-through'. This is to contrast it with the holding back of the right side in the traditional follow-through of the Hogan Swing, which robs the swing of its distance potential.)

These benefits of the very open left foot are key to unlocking the distance potential of a golf swing. *It redresses a major weakness of the Ben Hogan Swing.*

The Sum Effect is Greater than the Individual Principles

All three principles of the Convex Swing need to be applied simultaneously to realize the full distance potential of a golf swing.

The cumulative additive effect of the three mutually reinforcing principles enables the shaft to retain a convex shape throughout the impact zone before it impacts the ball with a convex bend or straight shaft. This is referred to as the Convex Strike on the golf ball.

The Convex Strike Force (CSF) on the ball can increase driving distance significantly, perhaps by 20%.

The Convex Strike Will Change the Game

The Convex Strike is truly disruptive. It can revolutionize the game of golf for decades to come, if not in perpetuity. For the simple reason that there is no third way to bend a golf shaft. And the convex bend is by far the stronger bend!

The Convex Strike is the ultimate *route* to the pursuit of ever greater distance.

Perhaps the Convex Strike, the means rather than distance in itself, is ultimately 'the Holy Grail of Golf.'

This grail all started with an idea posed as a question: "Why can't the convex bend of the shaft be used to propel a golf ball?" First postulated in the 2020 book *The Reflex Convex Swing*.

The journey to achieve the unprecedented Convex Strike on the ball is what this book is about. [7]

The pursuit of the Convex Strike, the ultimate Grail of Golf, begins now.

[1] https://www.pga.com/archive/news/pga/in-search-golfs-holy-grail-more-distance

[2] Driving distance over the past 40 years - PGA Tour https://www.pga.com/story/how-driving-distance-has-changed-over-the-past-40-years-on-the-pga-tour

[3] For convenience, it is referred to as an 'armpit-width' stance; this stance has its width the same as that of the shoulders. This should be referred to as the shoulder-width stance. But the use of 'armpit-width' serves to differentiate it from the established but mis-named Hogan 'shoulder-width' stance.

[4] The extent of the pre-turning of the feet depends on the suppleness and strength of the golfer. A supple golfer needs foot orientations that are pre-turned to a larger degree. The larger degree of turn in the right foot (45 degrees) enables a more compact backswing without compromising the energy generated. The more open left foot (90 degrees) turn does not block the momentum of the downswing; it facilitates a faster downswing.

[5] The 'fan-slide' movement of the sole of the left foot *off the ground* mimics that of an oriental fan as it opens, with the thin flat ribs sliding over each other as they pivot on the hinge of the fan.

(6) The X-Factor is notionally taken as 60 degrees as suggested in Ben Hogan's *Five Lessons* diagram on page 56. For Rory McIlory and Gordon Sargent, it can be about 64 degrees as estimated in https://youtu.be/6Tv0fjK7LqU?si=uuzbZVa17Yq8Cgw4

The X-Factor Stretch increases the angle between the shoulder and hip plane by 5 degrees: https://www.philcheetham.com/wp-content/uploads/2011/11/Stretching-the-X-Factor-Paper.pdf.

That increases the distance potential of a swing. For Gordon Sargent, the maximum X-Factor Stretch is about 70 degrees.

(7) For questions and comments, the author can be reached at: saifahcheong@gmail.com. He can coach anyone interested in acquiring the Convex Swing and attempting the Convex Strike. All you need to do is to take a video of your swing with a smartphone in slow motion mode. The author will guide you via email commentary. *No subscription or coaching fee is required.*

Notes:

- Many terms used in the text relate to those of a right-handed golfer for convenience and ease of description (with due apologies to left-handers). For example, an anti-clockwise movement, a left foot pivot, etc, are described from a right-hander's perspective.

- The reference to a golfer is neutral in gender. 'He' can be referred to as a 'She' or other for convenience of description.

- The contents of this book refer frequently to *The Reflex Convex Swing*, published by the author in 2020. The 2020 precursor book, a DIY guide, provides the background material to understand several ideas, some of which are presented briefly in this book. This reference to the 2020 book for detailed explanation is to limit the size of this book.

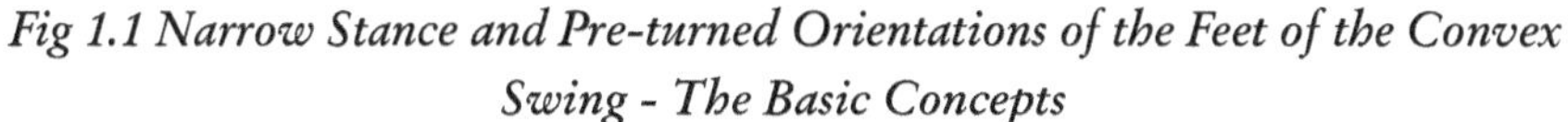

Fig 1.1 Narrow Stance and Pre-turned Orientations of the Feet of the Convex Swing - The Basic Concepts

- The width of the stance is narrow, where the distance between the inner heels is the same as that between the armpits. (This stance also has the distance between the outer heels as the width of the shoulders.)

- The right foot is turned 20 - 45 degrees toward the target.

- The left foot is turned 60 - 90 degrees toward the target.

- Both feet are oriented *anti-clockwise* to facilitate the *anti-clockwise* movement of the downswing (for a right-handed golfer).

- The rotational movement of the lower body is the primary motive force driving the downswing. This import from field sports blends seamlessly with and exploits the narrow stance and the pre-turned *anti-clockwise* foot positions. It pivots on the left heel while its sole fan-slides *off the ground*, resulting in a 'frictionless' movement that enhances the mechanical efficiency of the golf swing.

-24-

02

PROVING THE CONCEPT – THE CONVEX SWING

This journey began with Alex from Australia, a reader of my book *The Reflex Convex Swing*. He contacted me and expressed his enthusiasm about the ideas in the book. Being a student of Mindy Blake, he was naturally receptive. He asked to be coached to acquire the new reflex convex swing.

The author and his student communicated through photos of Alex's swing sequences and email exchanges. This process turned out to be economical and reasonably efficient.

Alex had modeled his swing on many elements of Mindy Blake's method. So, it was reasonably easy for him to understand and adopt several features of *The Reflex Convex Swing.*

Easy Changes to the Address Positions

The first change was to adopt a stance wider than Blake's but significantly narrower than Hogan's. This 'armpit-width' stance had the distance between the inner heels as that between the armpits. (This stance also has the distance between the outer heels as the width of the shoulders.) It was about six inches narrower than Hogan's shoulder-width stance. The 'armpit-width' stance was wide enough for the powerful rotational movement of the lower body to drive the downswing forcefully while remaining stable.

The second change was to assume that at the address, the 'radical' orientation of both feet turned *anti-clockwise* toward the target - the right foot was 20 degrees, and the left foot was 45 degrees. These orientations facilitated the *anti-clockwise* rotation of the downswing. That was easy to do as it was only a matter of getting used to them.

Backswing Needed to be Learned Anew

The changes to acquire a new backswing needed to be learned anew. The new focus was to use the left shoulder *solely* to push the left arm and club to execute the backswing. This was intended to suppress the instinctive use of the dominant right arm and hand in executing the backswing. Thus, it allowed the left shoulder, rather than the arm and hand, to dominate the backswing. It also allowed the left shoulder to coil more efficiently and forcefully against the right side, hip, and leg.

Alex, being a right-hander, had a weaker left side. His right arm and hand invariably helped to 'lift' the club up in the backswing. That upset the rhythm, shape, and connectedness of the backswing. The desired compact backswing could not be easily obtained.

He needed to strengthen the muscles of the left shoulder/side substantially. He needed to do the drills prescribed in Chapter 7 of *The Reflex Convex Swing*.

When equipped with sufficient strength, the left shoulder was able to push solely, firmly, and efficiently against the right hip, leg, and side. The left arm was kept relatively straight and relaxed.

The top of the backswing position was largely determined by the right foot pre-turned toward the target. When the right hip and leg were held sturdy by the right foot pre-turned 20 degrees, the backswing was compact with the left arm at the 10 o'clock position. The left arm and club pointed left of the target with the shaft at about 30 to 50 degrees above horizontal. This position required the right leg and side to have the strength to hold the body weight onto the inside edge of the right leg and hip.

The early sessions of training focused on acquiring a top of the backswing with the above-mentioned characteristics.

A good backswing, by and large, determined the outcome of the downswing.

New Drills to Get an Effective Downswing

Soon, it became necessary to perform exercises targeted at improving the strength of the rotational muscles of the lower body. The focus then turned to practicing the drills for an effective downswing, as described in Chapter 8 of *The Reflex Convex Swing*.

When the necessary strength was acquired, the focus was on pushing off the ball of the right foot to initiate the downswing. In this first move down, the rotational movement of the lower body instinctively transfers the bodyweight onto the *heel* of the pre opened 45-degree left foot.

When the rotational movement of the lower body became powerful enough, the left foot would pivot on its heel, and its sole would fan-slide *off the ground* to accommodate the momentum of the downswing. This 'pivot fan-slide' movement was first done by Audrey Ho Mei Lian.*

(*The term "pivot fan-slide" describes how an oriental fan opens with the thin, flat ribs sliding over each other as they pivot on the hinge of the fan. A collage of photos of Audrey Ho was sent to Alex to help him visualize and adopt that innovative movement.)

The above measures were implemented over a few months.

The result was a swing as good as many professional golf swings. The swing sequence can be viewed at https://youtu.be/cCtFdaR5Og4.

The Basic Convex Swing was Functional

Alex's effort provided the proof of concept that the reflex convex swing was viable, easy to learn, and play with.

Unfortunately, Alex was not able to achieve the Convex Strike on the ball. But he came tantalizingly close to doing so.

He needed, perhaps, another 10 to 20 percent rotational speed in the movement of the lower body.

The ball position was perhaps too far forward in his stance. Straightening his left leg at impact may have reduced the rotational speed somewhat.

The pursuit of the elusive Convex Strike remains.

The following chapters catalog the efforts made on that journey by another student to achieve the Convex Strike on the ball.

03

BUILDING STRENGTH FOR THE CONVEX STRIKE

The Convex Swing coaching YouTube, https://youtu.be/cCtFdaR5Og4, featuring Alex's swing, attracted the interest of YT Siew. YT was the illustrator of my book, *The Reflex Convex Swing*.

YT wanted to learn the Convex Swing and attempt the elusive Convex Strike on the ball. This prompted a fresh approach, addressing the problems encountered by Alex, the first student to play the Convex Swing.

Adopting a New Approach - Building Strength

The new approach focuses on equipping the body with the needed strength before learning to execute the two key movements of the golf swing.

The repetition of the key movements helps build the muscle memory to execute them reflexively.

The key movements of the Convex Swing are: (a) the left shoulder solely pushes the left arm and club to the top of the backswing, and (b) the rotational movement of the lower body predominantly powers the downswing.

Movement (a) generates the potential energy needed for an effective golf swing, without the instinctive use of the right arm.

Movement (b) transmits the energy stored in the backswing into a powerful swing force to propel the golf ball in the downswing.

Those muscles must be strengthened *before* they can be used to build an effective and efficient golf swing. This expedites the process of acquiring a good swing.

The new focus requires two sets of muscles to be strengthened: (1) the left side, shoulder, and arm, and (2) the rotational muscles of the lower body.

The first set determines the ability to generate the maximum potential energy for the swing. The second determines the ability to transmit the energy generated into a powerful downswing force.

A body, suitably strengthened physically, executes the crucial elements of the Convex Swing more readily, efficiently, and reflexively.

This approach of preconditioning the body movements has been used in other sports, like learning the basic badminton movements without hitting the shuttlecock or acquiring the twisting diving movements with a harness before actually diving in the water. However, this approach is rarely employed in learning the golf swing.

As it turned out, it has expedited the progress made by YT. *It pointed to a new and effective way to teach and acquire a golf swing.*

The basic exercises to prepare the body to execute the most important elements of the swing have been advocated in Chapters 7 and 8 of *The Reflex Convex Swing*. Some are reproduced below.

Strengthening the Left Shoulder, Arm, and Side

For most right-handers, the left side is the weaker side. YT is no exception. So, the priority is to strengthen the left side since it is the dominant side in a golf swing.

To execute a backswing properly, the left shoulder must solely be used to push the arm and club back in an inclined plane *without the help of the right arm.*

The right arm remains passive. It merely responds to the push of the left shoulder by folding naturally, as dictated by the push of the left shoulder.

The predominant use of the left shoulder and arm maintains the *connectedness in the dependent movements of the components* in the backswing[1]. The various components of the body stay connected and linked to each other in their relative orientation as set at the address. Throughout the backswing, the left arm remains close to the left chest; it does not rotate *independently* relative to the left shoulder via the shoulder joint.

By pushing *solely* with the left shoulder, the obtuse left arm/shaft angle assumed at the address remains so throughout the backswing until the top of the backswing is reached. There is no deliberate cocking of the wrists[2]. At the top of the backswing, the shaft of the club points skywards, left of the target line, and is about 30 degrees above horizontal.

Focusing *solely* on the left shoulder ensures that the backswing movement is deliberately slow since it is not natural to move the shoulder fast. In that way, the push of the left shoulder stretches fully the right leg and glute muscles while transferring the body weight predominantly to the *inside* of the right leg and foot.

A muscle that is stretched slowly can be stretched to a greater length. Up to a point, the more stretched it is, the more forceful its eventual contraction. When the big muscles of the core, back, and legs are slowly and fully stretched during the backswing, they generate and store the maximum energy available for the downswing.

YT had to strengthen his left side using a weighted club when doing Drill 1 of Chapter 7 of *The Reflex Convex Swing*. When the left shoulder and arm have acquired the needed strength, Drill 2 of Chapter 7 was used to train the right side and arm to be passive in executing the backswing.

These Drills are Reproduced Below:

Drill 1. Push solely with the left shoulder when doing the backswing.

This drill trains the left shoulder *solely* to initiate and perform the backswing without using the arms and hands (Figure 3.1).

1. Assume the address position (with the 'armpit-width' stance and both feet turned toward the target).

2. Hold the club in the left hand.

3. Rest the fingers of the right hand lightly on the left shoulder.

4. Bring the elbow of the bent right arm to the left arm*. (The folded right arm forms a triangle with the shoulders to restrain the left arm from moving independently of the left shoulder.)

5. Turn the left shoulder backward and upward along an inclined arc and inside the target line while keeping the 'bent right arm' triangle in contact with the left arm. (The left shoulder pushes the left arm and club backward and upward. Throughout this movement, focus on the neck being the center of the inclined arc and the head remaining steady, both

vertically and laterally. The head-neck axis tilts as it follows the tilting of the shoulder plane.)

6. Continue to turn and push the left shoulder until the right leg and glute muscles are taut at the top of the backswing*. (In the process, ensure the right leg is bent, and its knee is held sturdy by the resisting right thigh muscles to prevent the body weight from swaying outside the right heel. At the top of the backswing, the pressure of the body weight is felt at the ball of the right foot and the inside edge of the right heel.)

7. Relax and repeat.

(*The left arm does not move independently of the left shoulder. It is not deliberately lifted when the left shoulder stops pushing against the right side at the top of the backswing. Any deliberate 'lifting' of the left arm alters the orientation of the left arm relative to the left chest set at the address. The left arm becomes disconnected from the shoulder. When that happens, conscious corrective actions are necessary during the downswing, often with limited success. Hence, playing by reflex is compromised.)

Initially, the golfer may not be able to push the left arm too far back. With training, a supple golfer can get the left arm (while holding a weighted club) to horizontal with a right foot turned 20 - 30 degrees toward the target.

This drill strengthens the muscles of the left shoulder, side, and arm. If the left side needs to be strengthened appreciably, practice the same drill with a weighted club. A dumbbell may be used, but it does not benefit from the 'moment of inertia' effect of a weighted club.

A strengthened left shoulder and arm structure is necessary to curb the instinctive use of the right side in the backswing. Since the backswing influences the downswing a great deal, this simple drill will yield enormous benefits.

Repeated exercise over time results in increased strength of the left shoulder/side. This increased strength of the left side interactively increases the resisting strength of the right foot/leg and side. The net effect is an increase in the energy generated in the backswing as elaborated on in Chapter 4.

The strong resisting strength of the right side holds the right foot/leg/hip sturdy. It allows the right side to push off the ball of the right foot aggressively to initiate the downswing and to rotate the body weight onto the left heel, as elaborated on in Chapter 5.

Thus, this is the most effective drill to master the most important move in a connected backswing!

It focuses on only one key - the push of the left shoulder - to perform the backswing.

Fig 3.1 Pushing with the Left Shoulder and Strengthening the Left Side

- Assume the address position (with the 'armpit-width' stance and both feet turned toward the target).

- Hold the club with the left hand.

- Bring the fingers of the right hand to touch the left shoulder while the *elbow of the right arm is in contact with the lower left arm just below the left elbow.* (This also ensures that the left arm remains straight while doing the backswing.)

- Push the club back with the left shoulder while the right elbow remains in contact with the lower left arm.

- The picture shows that the left shoulder has pushed the left arm to about 30 degrees from horizontal and the right leg and glute muscles are stretched with the right knee held sturdy at its address position. (It may be difficult to push any higher until the muscles of the left side and arm are strengthened. Only then should a higher backswing be attempted for the left arm to reach left shoulder height or to the top of the backswing.)

Drill 2. Keep the right hand grip pressure light (i.e., with zero pressure).

With the necessary strength acquired through Drill 1, the left shoulder can push the left arm to the 10 o'clock position *without using the right arm*. This prevents the right arm from being activated too early, if at all, in the downswing; it is an important key to acquiring a reflex swing.

This drill is designed to keep the right arm and hand passive during the backswing.

1. Assume the address position (with the 'armpit-width' stance and both feet turned toward the target).

2. Hold the club in the left hand.

3. Bring the right hand to grip the club in the usual way.

4. Relax the right hand grip until the fingers and palm exert no pressure on the club.

5. Use only the left shoulder to push the left arm and club back on an inclined plane.

6. Keep the pressure of the right hand grip as light (close to zero pressure) as possible and for as long into the backswing as possible.[#]

7. Keep pushing the left shoulder backward and upward until the left arm reaches the 10 o'clock position (which is the

top of the backswing). Along the way, *the left arm needs to remain relaxed*; a tense left arm suggests that the left shoulder muscles are not strong enough to do the backswing properly.

8. Allow the obtuse arm/shaft angle at the address to remain so during the backswing until the top of the backswing is reached.

9. Relax and repeat.

(# To capture the correct feeling, the drill can be repeated with only the middle fingers of the right hand touching but not grabbing the club. If the backswing cannot be done with only the left shoulder pushing the arm and club, repeat Drill 1 to strengthen the left side, shoulder, and arm.)

At or near the top of the backswing, the right arm must not be tense, and the pressure of the right hand grip must remain light.

When the right arm and hand are kept out of the backswing, the obtuse left arm/shaft angle at the address remains obtuse. At the top of the backswing, the shaft is about 30 degrees above the horizontal and points skywards left of the target line. ^

(^ Any use of the right arm, consciously or subconsciously, to manipulate the club during the backswing causes the shaft to point more toward and even cross the target line. When that happens, conscious corrective actions are needed during the downswing, thereby making it less consistent.)

Strengthening the Rotational Muscles - Drills

Strengthening the muscles of the left shoulder and side is critical to building an effective backswing. The backswing generates the potential energy for the golf swing.

The energy generated is stored in the rotational muscles of the backswing. It is then transmitted into a powerful strike force in the downswing. The rotational movement of the lower body transmits that power through the core muscles to the left side and upper body. In turn, the left shoulder and arm drag the club along throughout the impact zone to strike the ball.

The faster the lower body rotates, the more likely the convex bend of the shaft is retained throughout the impact zone. **Thus, the strength of the rotational muscles holds the key to striking the ball with a convex bend shaft.**

The strength of the rotational muscles can be obtained through appropriate gym work.

For recreational golfers, the rotational speed of the lower body can also be acquired through a series of exercises using rubber tubes that can be done conveniently at home. The inner tubes of racing bicycles are suitable for these exercises.

The exercises below *simulate* the backswing and downswing movements. The fitness of the golfer determines the number of tubes used to provide the necessary resistance suitable for the intended number of repetitions for each set.

For each exercise:

1. Anchor enough rubber tubes to a pillar or joint to provide the needed resistance.
2. Assume the Convex Swing 'armpit-width' stance.
3. Turn the right foot 30-45 degrees toward the target.
4. Turn the left foot 60-90 degrees toward the target.
5. Stretch the rubber tubes to the required tension to begin each exercise.

6. Perform the rotational movements *slowly* for better effect.

7. In a backswing exercise, focus on pushing **solely** with the left shoulder and side.

8. In a downswing exercise, focus on pushing off the **ball** of the right foot to initiate the rotational movement of the lower body. Then, rotate the left hip/thigh to shift the body weight onto the left heel (and not the ball) of the left foot.

The effectiveness of the exercises manifests itself in the bulging of the muscles of the inner right leg, the outer left leg/thigh, around the left hip, and the glutes. The muscles of the left leg from the inner ankle straddling the left shin to the left knee also become more prominent. The rotational muscles become stronger and taut as progress is made.

Drill 1 - Turn the left shoulder to coil against the right side, as in the backswing

1. Pull the rubber tubes (with the left hand and arm bent at the elbow) across the back shoulders and around the backswing axis.

2. Position the tubes between the left shoulder joint and the upper portion of the left arm to cover the shoulder blade.

3. Move away from the pillar/anchor to stretch the tubes to a suitable tension.

4. Place the right hand securely on the right thigh.

5. Rotate the left shoulder/side clockwise against the right leg/ side.

6. Relax and repeat.

Drill 2 - Turn the left hip/shoulder/upper body against the right hip/ leg, as in the backswing

1. Pull the rubber tubes with the right hand around the right hip and across the buttocks at the hip/waist level. Then, hold the free ends of the tubes with the left hand and anchor the left hand (holding the tubes securely) at the back of the left hip.

2. Move away from the pillar/anchor to stretch the tubes to a suitable tension.

3. Rotate the left hip/shoulder/upper body clockwise against the right hip/leg/side. (To help the left shoulder turn, hold the left shoulder with the right hand and rotate the left shoulder against the right hip.)

4. Feel the torsion on the *inside* of the right leg/hip, the rotational stretch of the right thigh, and the tension of the glute muscles.

5. Relax and repeat.

Drill 3 - Push off the *ball* of the right foot and Rotate the hips, as in starting a downswing

1. Pull the rubber tubes away with the right hand and the right arm bent at the elbow.

2. Position and rest the right elbow at the right hip joint.

3. Move away from the pillar/anchor to stretch the tubes to a suitable tension.

4. Push off the *ball* of the right foot and rotate the right hip anti-clockwise toward the left leg/side.

5. Rotate the right hip with the hip plane tilted about 30 degrees as in a normal downswing movement.

6. Rotate the right hip around the swing axis *until the hip plane is more than 90 degrees away from the target line.*

7. Feel the torsional stretch on the outside of the entire left leg and hip.

8. Relax and repeat.

Drill 4 - Use the right hip/leg to drive the left upper body and left arm, as in a downswing

1. Wrap the free ends of the rubber tubes around the left wrist.

2. Position the left arm at the 7 o'clock position with the left hand at the right hip.

3. Move away from the pillar/anchor to stretch the tubes to a suitable tension.

4. Push off the *ball* of the right foot and Rotate the right hip/leg anti-clockwise toward the left hip/leg *until the hip plane is more than 90 degrees from the target line.*

5. Feel the torsional stretch on the outside of the left leg/hip and the left upper body.

6. Relax and repeat.

Drill 5 - Rotate the left shoulder and left arm to a full follow-through

1. Place the tubes around the left shoulder, under the armpit, and across the left chest.

2. Move away from the anchor to stretch the tubes to a suitable tension.

3. Push off the ball of the right foot and rotate the right hip/leg anti-clockwise toward the left hip/leg *until the hip plane is more than 90 degrees away from the target line.*

4. Rotate *simultaneously* the left shoulder and upper body anti-clockwise around the body axis to a full finish.

5. Relax and repeat.

While the drills of the backswing and downswing are listed sequentially, it may be useful to do them alternatively to allow for rest and recovery of the muscles involved.

Training the Swing Without Striking the Ball

As in many sports, the basic movements are best developed by practicing the motions without the distracting influence of the sport's object, like the shuttlecock in badminton or the ball in tennis or golf. Or practicing the twisting diving movements with a harness before diving into the pool.

Many know how it is to swing a club smoothly with rhythmic power. Yet not many spend enough time to do so without a ball.

YT chose to build a swing doing just that, namely swinging a driver or a 5-wood without striking a ball.

After strengthening his body with the exercises described in the preceding sections, he began to mimic the full swing with a driver or a 5-wood.

At each session, he approached each swing as if he were striking an imaginary ball, positioned at the middle of his stance and marked by a tee or a peg on the practice mat. At the address, he would adopt the 'armpit-width' stance and turn the right foot 45 degrees and the left 90 toward the target. (Initially, he started with a left foot turned 60 degrees toward the target. But the eventual 90 degrees pre-turned left foot makes it easier to pivot on the left heel.)

He would consciously push *solely* with his left shoulder to take the left arm and club back on an inclined plane to arrive at the correct top of the backswing position. Every so often, he checks the top of the backswing position for these characteristics:

1. The body weight is on the *inside* edges of the right foot and leg. The toe and the ball of the right foot remain on the ground. (These measures ensure that there is no swaying of the body away from the swing axis to the outside edge of the right leg/foot.)

2. The left arm is at the 10 or 9 o'clock position, depending on the pre-turned angle of the right foot. (There is no deliberate and independent lifting of the left arm when the left shoulder stops turning against the right side.)

3. The club shaft is pointed skywards and left of the target line. The left arm/shaft angle remains obtuse as at the address. (A shaft pointed more toward the target line must be avoided; it would have been manipulated by the cocking of the right hand and wrist and/or the rotation of the left arm via the shoulder joint. Such movements, done deliberately or subconsciously, disrupts the connectedness in the backswing, leading to inconsistency.)

4. The left arm covers the right shoulder when viewed down the line. (This ensures that the left shoulder has pushed the left arm and shaft on the correct inclined swing plane.)

From the top of the backswing, he would push off aggressively with the *ball* of the right foot and rotate the lower body as hard and as fast as he possibly could. When the rotational speed of the lower body is high enough, his right leg revolves around the left leg and lands his right foot across the target line on rotational follow-through, as a shot putter would continue his rotational momentum on follow-through*. The extent of the right leg revolving around the left leg is determined by the rotational speed of the lower body. (*For convenience, this movement is referred to as rotational follow-through. This is to distinguish it from the restricted follow-through of the Hogan Swing.)

In the downswing, he focuses on shifting the body weight onto the left heel, pivoting on the left heel, and rotating the lower body around the swing axis. Consequently, the sole of the left foot fan-slides *off the ground* and points well left of the target line when completing the swing.

In a truly efficient swing, the whole body pivots on the left heel and revolves around the swing axis; the right leg revolves around the left leg and lands the foot across the target line, the extent of which is determined by the residual rotational follow-through momentum left in the swing.

Throughout the downswing, he focuses on retaining the bend in the left leg for as long as possible throughout the impact zone. (A straight left leg is inimical to rotational movement.)

Throughout the swing, and particularly during the downswing, he maintains eye contact with the peg or tee, marking the ball position. By doing so, the shoulder plane becomes more tilted at the top of the backswing and throughout the downswing, especially at the impact position. The head-neck axis moves in a circular arc in tandem with the shoulders.

This emphasis on maintaining eye contact with the peg or tee is instrumental in achieving an impact position *where the shoulder plane is tilted and the left arm remains close to the chest.*

Are These Exercises Sufficient?

The efficacy of the exercises can be judged by the ability to produce the Convex Strike on the ball (as described in Chapter 9).

With the appropriate exercises, such as those in this chapter or with appropriate gym workouts, the Convex Swing System allows more golfers to aspire to strike the ball with a convex bend shaft.

That notwithstanding, it needs to be stressed that the Convex Strike is made easier by the many enabling features of the Convex Swing System. *These features reduce the threshold rotational swing speed to obtain the Convex Strike.* They enhance the probability of achieving the Convex Strike by more golfers.

Thus, the enabling features of the Convex Swing System are discussed in the next several chapters. Collectively, they accentuate the overall effectiveness and efficiency of the Convex Swing.

(1) Pushing *solely* with the left shoulder determines the natural width of the backswing arc. The width of the natural arc is characterized by the golfer's stature. *Any conscious attempt to increase the width of this natural arc must be avoided.* Like pushing the left arm further away from the left chest or increasing the obtuse left arm/shaft angle set at the address. Such conscious attempts will reduce the connectedness in the dependent movements of the components of the backswing, resulting in an inconsistent backswing to the detriment of playing by reflex.

(2) When the right arm and hand are not passive in executing the backswing, the wrists become cocked at the top of the backswing. When combined with a deliberate 'lifting' of the left arm at the

top of the backswing, this action can cause the shaft of the club to point more toward the target line or even across it. This reduces the connectedness in the dependent movements of the components of the backswing, resulting in an inconsistent downswing.

04

GENERATING MORE ENERGY IN THE BACKSWING

The main purpose of the backswing is to generate the potential energy for the swing to propel the golf ball.

The maximum amount of energy that can be generated in the backswing depends on how efficiently and how hard the left shoulder/side pushes against the right side. The harder the left shoulder pushes, the more the right side needs to resist. These two movements *interactively* strengthen progressively the muscles of both the left and right sides.

Over time, with practice and repetition, as the muscles strengthen, the amount of energy that can be generated in the backswing increases. (Needless to say, an increase in strength in those muscles can be obtained through appropriate gym work.)

While the energy generated increases progressively, the maximum angle between the shoulder and the hip plane remains about 60 degrees for most golfers. This is the X-Factor in golf parlance. It occurs at the completion of the backswing. It does not depend on the length of the backswing. (The pre-turning of the right foot toward the target at the address primarily determines the length of the backswing.)

That maximum angle between the shoulder and hip planes can be achieved efficiently when the right hip/leg/side is held sturdy with a right foot pre-turned toward the target. The more the right foot is pre-turned toward the target, the less the left shoulder needs to turn around the swing axis.

A right foot turned 20 - 45 degrees toward the target allows the left shoulder to position the left arm at 10 or 9 o'clock at the top of the backswing, depending on the strength and suppleness of the golfer.

A short backswing obtained by a pre-turned right foot does not compromise the amount of energy generated in a backswing.

The maximum amount of energy that can be generated resides in the strength of the stretched muscles of the left side pushing against those of the right side. Indeed, a short backswing promotes the efficiency of energy generation because the maximum X-Factor is obtained earlier.

A short backswing with less shoulder turn around the swing axis is less prone to error, leading to a more consistent backswing.

Making an Efficient Backswing

To execute the backswing properly, the left shoulder must solely be used to push the left arm and club in an upward-inclined arc *without the right arm helping the movement in any way* (Figure 4.1).

While being pushed along that inclined arc, the left arm must not rotate independently around the shoulder joint; this is to maintain the orientation of the left arm to the chest established at the address. This maintains the *connectedness* in the movements of the components in the backswing. [1]

During the backswing, the obtuse left arm/shaft angle established at the address remains obtuse until it reaches the top of the backswing. The wrists must not be deliberately cocked to obtain an acute arm/shaft angle (or combined with the deliberate 'lifting' of the left arm) to lengthen the backswing. [2]

Starting with an obtuse angle at the top of the backswing, the drive of the lower body can change it to acute later into the downswing. In that way, the convex bend of the shaft can occur later and, as a result, can be maintained further into the impact zone and nearer to impact on the ball.

Fig 4.1 Backswing - Push with the Left shoulder

- The left shoulder *solely* pushes the left arm and club to the top of the backswing. The right arm folds at the elbow naturally, responding to the push of the left shoulder and left arm.

- The right arm/hand remains *passive* throughout the backswing.

- The picture shows the left arm holding the butt of the club at right hip height with the left and right wrist angles still at their natural address positions.

- With a passive right arm not cocking the left wrist, the left arm/ shaft angle remains obtuse when the top of the backswing is reached.

- During the backswing, the left arm remains relaxed. It stops moving as the left shoulder stops pushing against the right side when it reaches the top of the backswing. At the top, the left arm and shaft must not move independently any further so as to retain the connectedness between the components in the backswing. At the top of the backswing, *the left arm/shaft angle remains obtuse.*

The Convex Swing Generates Energy Efficiently

In the Convex Swing System, the push of the left shoulder against the right hip/side can generate the maximum energy with a short backswing. This maximum energy is generated in a number of ways.

First, over a narrow 'armpit-width' stance, the left shoulder revolves easily around the axis of the swing. The body weight stays within the confines of the inner right foot, leg, and hip. It does not sway further to the outside of the right foot. The pressure is felt on the ball, the inner heel of the right foot, and the inner edge of the right leg.

Second, the right foot pre-turned toward the target holds the right leg and hip sturdy. To be effective, the right knee needs to be kept at its address position as much as possible. This allows the left shoulder to stretch immediately the muscles of the right side as soon as it starts pushing. *The slower the stretch, the more energy is generated.*

With the right foot and knee held sturdy, the stretch of the muscles is felt in the right thigh, hip, and glute. There is very little movement of the right hip. The right leg remains bent with the thigh muscles engaged but not tense.

To hold the right side firmly, the right foot needs to be turned at the address toward the target at least 20 degrees. For the supple golfer, a 30 to 45-degree turn is preferred to achieve a more compact backswing.

A more pronounced pre-turned right foot confers an additional benefit; *it helps a golfer push off the ball of the foot more effectively in the downswing.* It is more efficient than pushing with the instep. Such an action is closer to a 100m sprinter pushing with the ball of his foot against the starter block.

The more aggressive push off the ball of the right foot rotates the left hip early and plants the body weight firmly onto the left heel as the backswing is being completed. The subsequent rotation of the lower body pivots on the heel (and not on the ball) of the left foot and drives the left hip/leg around the swing axis. In that way, the early movement of the left hip/leg *stretches* the X-Factor to exceed 60 degrees, thereby increasing the energy available in the downswing.

Third, the left shoulder only needs to push a short distance before it can push no further against the right side while keeping the body weight on the inside edge of the right foot and leg. The inner edge and the toe of the right foot stay on the ground to prevent overswinging.

Such a compact backswing can be done more reliably than a longer one.

Checkpoints of a well-executed Backswing

The top of a well-executed backswing is shown in (Figure 4.2). The positions of various components remain connected in their orientations preset at the address. (This illustration is reproduced, with some modifications, from *The Reflex Convex Swing*.)

The checkpoints of a well-executed backswing are:

1. Most of the body weight, 80 to 90 percent, is transferred to the right side.

2. The stretch of the muscles of the right side must be felt throughout the right leg (in the thigh/hip/glute muscles) and onto the ball of the right foot. The pressure is felt on the *inside* edge of the right foot and leg. The ball of the right foot remains on the ground.

3. The right knee remains at its address position as much as possible, and the right leg is suitably flexed with the thigh muscles engaged but not tense.

4. The glute muscles of the right hip are engaged.

5. The left arm is at a 10 o'clock position or lower. The arm is essentially straight, with as little bend at the elbow as possible, but not tense. (*When viewed down the line, the left arm covers the right shoulder, indicative of the desired shoulder plane tilt and swing plane.*)

6. The shaft of the club is pointed skyward and left of the target and about 30 to 50 degrees above horizontal. The left arm/shaft angle remains obtuse at the top of the backswing.

7. The angle between the shoulder and the hip plane is at a maximum. This is the much sought-after X-Factor of about 60 degrees for the supple golfer.

8. The components of the swing are Connected, the muscles are Taut, and the structure of the backswing is Compact. This is the **CTC** top of the backswing position.

To maximize the generation of energy, the push of the left shoulder needs to be deliberate and slow. When done slowly, the muscles are stretched more efficiently. Muscles that are well-stretched store the most amount of energy. They also contract efficiently and produce the maximum force.

The strength of the left shoulder and side is crucial to determining the maximum amount of energy generated in the backswing. When the left side/shoulder pushes the right side progressively harder, it strengthens the resisting muscles of the right side. These two movements interactively, over time, result in a higher amount of energy generated in the backswing.

A stronger left shoulder allows the left arm to be more relaxed during the backswing. The right arm is passive, merely folding in response to the sole push of the left shoulder.

This dominance of the left shoulder needs to be stressed since a well-executed backswing has a major influence on the outcome of the downswing.

With maximum energy thus generated in the backswing, the next focus is on transmitting that potential energy into a powerful downswing force.

[1] A detailed description of the setup procedure for establishing a suitable posture and stance, connecting the body components in their preset orientations, and executing the backswing can be found in Chapters 4 and 6 of *The Reflex Convex Swing.*

A proper setup enables a simple, single-pushing movement of the left shoulder to initiate and achieve connectedness in the backswing. With the swing centered around the neck, the left shoulder naturally turns inwards and upwards on an inclined plane. This focus on a single key facilit*ates the automatic acquisition of the top of the backswing* without the distracting thoughts of consciously sequencing various dependent movements and achieving specific positions along the way.

The swing plane is determined by the posture at the address, where the components are connected in their orientations to each other as set during the address. In a well-executed backswing, *the left arm covers the right shoulder when viewed down the line,* determining the appropriate tilt of the shoulder plane for the golfer.

(2) The swing arc of the left arm and club shaft is determined by the push of the left shoulder on an inclined plane. At the top of the backswing, the left arm and club point skywards and naturally to the left of the target line.

Any deliberate or subconscious cocking of the wrists and/or lifting of the left arm after the left shoulder stops pushing at the top of the backswing must be avoided. Such action can cause the shaft to move more toward or even cross the target line, altering the swing plane determined by the push of the left shoulder where all the components are connected. Deliberate or subconscious wrist cocking results in an inconsistent downswing.

Fig 4.2 Top of Backswing (CTC) Position Checkpoints

- The right foot is turned 20-45 degrees toward the target, and the left foot 60-90 degrees.

- The right knee is kept at its address position as much as possible.

- The left shoulder is not naturally or necessarily under the chin.

- The left arm is at the 10 o'clock position, depending on the pre-turned angle of the right foot.

- The shaft of the club is 40-60 degrees above horizontal, pointing skyward and away from the back of the golfer and 40-60 degrees left of the target line.

- When viewed down the line, the left arm covers the right shoulder.

- The left arm/shaft angle remains obtuse at the top of the backswing.

- Most of the body weight, perhaps 80 to 90 percent, is on the inside of the right leg and foot.

- The big muscles of the right leg and the left upper body are fully coiled.

- The left leg has not moved much from its address position.

- The stretch felt in the inner muscles of the right leg and also in the outer muscles of the left leg makes it instinctive to initiate the downswing.

- The picture shows the structure is Connected, muscles Taut, and swing Compact.

05

TRANSMITTING THE POWER
OVER A SHORT ROUTE

The purpose of a backswing is to generate the potential energy to power the downswing.

The downswing transmits the generated potential energy into a powerful swing force to propel the ball as far as possible.

Every component and feature of the Convex Swing System facilitates that objective.

The rotational movement of the lower body over a narrow stance—a well-established field sports technique—is the most efficient way to transmit the stored energy into a powerful downswing force. *It is the primary power motive source that drives the Convex Swing.*

To achieve the Convex Strike on the ball, the rotational movement of the lower body must always *lead* the downswing. It must be fast enough to *retain* the convex bend of the shaft *throughout* the impact zone before it strikes the ball.

A Short Swing retains a Convex Bend shaft Better

The Convex Swing System pre-turns the right foot at the address 20 to 45 degrees toward the target to achieve the desired short backswing. At the top of the backswing, the left arm is at the 10 to 9 o'clock corresponding position. The structure of the backswing is compact.

The short backswing allows the first move down to transfer the body weight onto the left heel more readily. A short backswing needs a shorter time to impact; the shaft stays convex longer throughout the impact zone.

The more compact backswing of the Convex Swing is instrumental to the objective of obtaining a Convex Strike on the ball.

Shorter Route to Impact

In the Ben Hogan Swing, the top of the backswing has the left arm at the 12 o'clock position. From there, the downswing takes *three* '10-minute' clock face movements of the left arm to reach impact at the 6 o'clock position.

By contrast, the left arm of the Convex Swing at the completion of the backswing is at the 10 o'clock position. Thus, it needs to travel only *two* '10-minute' clock face movements to reach impact at the ball at 6 o'clock.

The Convex Swing only needs two-thirds (or 67%) of the time and distance to impact the ball. That will increase its chance of presenting a convex bend shaft to strike the ball.

A more supple golfer can pre-turn the right foot 45 degrees toward the target; the left arm at the top of the backswing is then at the 9 o'clock position. In this case, the left arm needs to travel *only*

15 minutes or less to impact. That is halving the time and distance required by the Hogan Swing.

Transmitting the Power over a Short Distance and Time

A motion control study on muscle contraction has shown that power output first increases at low velocities, peaks at intermediate velocities, and then gradually declines to zero. Maximum power is generated at approximately one-third of maximum muscle shortening velocity.[1]

A similar relationship should apply between power output and velocity during the stretching and contraction of muscles involved in a golf swing.

This suggests that maximum power in a golf swing is reached over a short distance or time before it declines.

This applies to professional golfers using the Hogan Swing. From the top of the backswing (12 o'clock position), the shaft transitions from straight to a convex bend when the left arm reaches the 8 o'clock position. The convexity of the shaft bend suggests the output has peaked (or is peaking) in the swing. This occurs in the first two '10-minute' movements of the left arm in the downswing. Thereafter, the swing slows because it is difficult to maintain the acceleration or power into the third '10-minute' movement. This deceleration is also exacerbated by the insufficiently open left foot, which actively impedes the downswing movement in this third segment.

In the third '10-minute' movement, from the left arm at 8 o'clock to impact at 6 o'clock, the swing slows down relatively. The shaft transitions from convex to straight and then to concave before impacting the ball. This phenomenon is similar to a 100m sprinter accelerating through the first 50m before maintaining his speed and slowing down thereafter.[2]

Consequently, *all professional golfers have thus far struck the golf ball with a concave bend shaft.*

By contrast, in the Convex Swing, the left arm needs to travel through *only two* '10-minute' movements to impact the ball—from the 10 o'clock top of the backswing position to the 6 o'clock impact position.

In addition, the downswing movement of the Convex Swing System is facilitated by a pre-turned, very open left foot and the 'pivot fan-slide' *off the ground* movement[3]. Therefore, it is relatively easier to retain the convex bend in the shaft throughout the shorter impact zone.

Holding a Convex Bend in the Shaft for 20 Minutes

All professional golfers have demonstrated the ability to hold a convex bend in the shaft through the first two '10-minute' movements. Thus, they can undoubtedly retain the convex bend to impact the ball when they adopt the shorter route of the Convex Swing.

The three and two '10-minute' segments traversed respectively by the Hogan Swing and the Convex Swing are shown in Figure 5.1. The diagrams show the change in the bend of the shaft at the various left arm positions in the downswing.

The Hogan Swing (the left diagram) has the shaft transitioning from convex to straight and then to concave before striking the ball.

The Convex Swing (the right diagram) maintains the convex bend of the shaft in the shorter 20-minute route to impact. With the shorter route, there is less time for the swing to slow down and allow the shaft to transition to a concave bend before striking the ball.*

(*The shaft does lose its convexity as it approaches the ball and most likely strikes the ball with a straight shaft. This is because it takes a truly high rotational speed of the lower body to maintain a convex bend to strike the ball. In practice, the shaft is most likely straight when captured on video, because the rolling shutter effect makes a shaft seem less convex than it actually is.)

All professional golfers have enough power in their swings to hold a convex bend for two '10-minute' segments. Therefore, they have the capacity to strike the ball with a convex bend shaft when they adopt the Convex Swing System.

All they need to do is adopt at least two if not all three, core principles of the Convex Swing System.[4] (The falsifiability of this statement can be readily tested by any professional golfer. There is no need for an extended debate on this matter. Just do the Karl Popper Test.[4])

To a professional golfer, executing the Convex Strike is a forgone conclusion, a gimme in golf.

The shorter route of the Convex Swing also makes it easier for amateur golfers to gain distance off the tee. Those with a high enough swing speed can achieve the Convex Strike, too.

The benefits of adopting and applying the core principles of the Convex Swing System are elaborated upon in the next several chapters.

[1] It is easier to retain power over a shorter route and time. This self evident notion is supported by a motion control study: https://courses.lumenlearning.com/boundless-ap/chapter/control-of-muscle-tension/

It finds: (1) The force a muscle generates is dependent on the length of the muscle and its shortening velocity; (2) Maximum power is generated at approximately one-third of maximum shortening velocity.

[2] A 100m sprinter accelerates through the first 50m before slowing down.

http://speedendurance.com/2008/08/22/usain-bolt-

100m-10-meter-splits-and-speed-endurance/

[3] The 'pivot fan-slide' move confers many benefits. These are elaborated upon in Chapter 7 of this book.

[4] Falsifiability is a deductive standard of evaluation of scientific theories and hypotheses, introduced by the philosopher of science Karl Popper in his book The Logic of Scientific Discovery (1934). A theory or hypothesis is falsifiable (or refutable) if it can be logically contradicted by an empirical test.

Fig 5.1 Length of Route to Impact - Hogan V Convex Swing

Shape of Shaft based on Left Arm position in the downswing

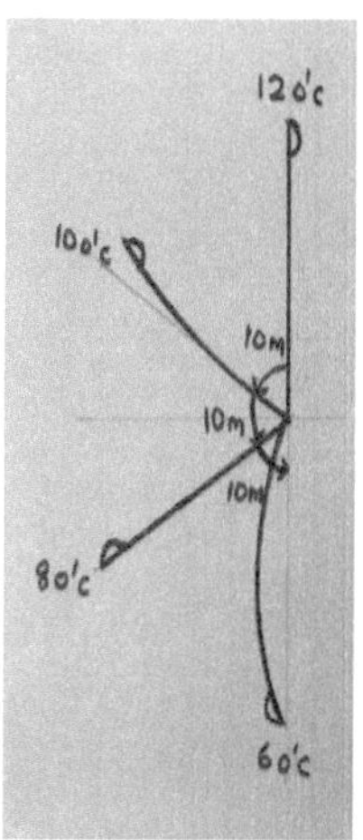

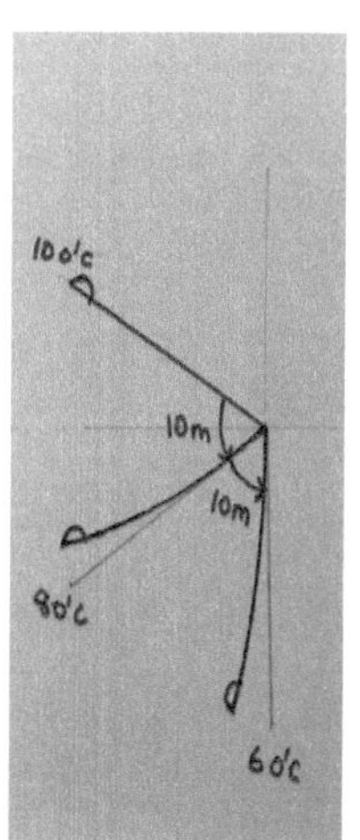

Hogan Swing   **Convex Swing**

	Hogan Swing	Convex Swing
Backswing		
Right foot	Square	Turned 20 degrees
Top of Backswing - Left arm	12 o'clock	10 o'clock
Angle between shoulder and hip plane	60 degrees	60 degrees
Energy generated	Maximum	Maximum
Downswing		
Stance - Distance between inner heels	Shoulder-width	Armpit-width
Left foot	22 degrees	45 - 60 degrees
Left arm movement to impact	30 minutes	20 minutes
Left foot's influence on momentum	Impedes	Facilitates
Shape of shaft at/near impact	Concave	Convex

06

APPLYING THE CORE PRINCIPLES

Achieving the Convex Strike on the ball has obviously been a daunting task. To this end, every golfer, professional or recreational, needs to employ all means at his disposal.

The three core principles of the Convex Swing System are designed for distance; they facilitate the objective of a Convex Strike, the ultimate route to acquire distance.

These core principles first propagated in *The Reflex Convex Swing*, are reiterated below:

1. Adopt the narrow 'armpit-width' stance at the address. The stance has the distance between the inner heels as that between the armpits[1]. (It is about six inches narrower than Hogan's 'shoulder-width' stance.)

2. Turn both feet at the address toward the target to facilitate the anti-clockwise movement of the downswing. The right foot is turned 20 - 45 degrees and the left foot 60 - 90 degrees. (In particular, the left foot needs to be very open so that it does not block the momentum of the rotational movement of the downswing.)

3. Use the rotational movement of the lower body as the prime motive source to power the golf swing. This movement is facilitated by a very open left foot pivoting on its heel and its sole fan-sliding *off the ground*. It is a 'frictionless' movement that enhances the rotational efficiency of the golf swing. (This is a well-known and used technique in field sports.)

These three principles are mutually reinforcing and cumulatively additive. In other words, their combined effect is greater than the sum of the individual components. **These principles are necessary and sufficient conditions to achieve the Convex Strike.** The chance of obtaining a Convex Strike can be significantly reduced if the three principles are not used *simultaneously*.

The rotational movement of the lower body occurs efficiently over a narrow stance. The *anti-clockwise* rotational movement of the lower body is facilitated by both feet pre-oriented *anti-clockwise* toward the target. The left foot pivot fan-slide synchronizes the *anti-clockwise* rotational movements throughout the impact zone. All these elements trade on each other to improve the mechanical efficiency of the golf swing.

The combined effect can produce a significantly longer distance off the tee by perhaps 20 percent. This potential increase in distance is phenomenal compared to the meager 5% increase in driving distance of the top professional golfers over the last two decades.

It is pertinent to note that none of the professional golfers has used all three core principles *simultaneously*. That probably accounts for the fact that the Convex Strike has not been done thus far. This is not to say that the professionals do not have the power and resources to do so.

It emphasizes that at least two, if not all three, enabling principles need to be used for the Convex Strike to occur.

The Pivot Fan-slide Improves the Efficiency of the Swing

The pivot fan-slide 'frictionless' movement plays a big part in the Convex Swing. It is deployed throughout the impact zone.

Bryson DeChambeau employed the pivot fan-slide movement recently when he remodeled his swing. He probably used it because the powerful momentum of his downswing dictated it. This was to allow him to complete his powerful follow-through swing; otherwise, he would have damaged his left knee.

If DeChambeau had intentionally used the pivot fan-slide movement with a left foot pre-turned to 60 - 90 degrees toward the target at the address, he could have done the convex strike on the ball. Maybe? Perhaps not.

But if he had adopted the other two or three core principles, he would definitely have achieved the Convex Strike on the ball. He would have added at least 20% to his distance off the tee rather than the modest 7% gain in distance from his enhanced physique and swing change (Golf Digest - Dan Rapaport Feb 06, 2022).[2]

The pivot fan-slide needs to be deployed *throughout* the impact zone.

Its many-faceted influence on the Convex Swing is elaborated upon in the next chapter.

[1] The Convex Swing 'armpit-width' stance also has the distance between the outer heels as the width of the shoulders. This can be referred to as the 'new' shoulder-width stance. The Hogan stance is effectively wider than the width of the shoulders since shoulders are within the distance between the inner heels. Thus it is a misnomer to call it a shoulder-width stance.

[2] Byrson DeChambeau gained 7 percent in driving distance from 2018 to 2021 after he rebuilt his swing and enhanced his physique.

https://www.golfdigest.com/story/bryson-dechambeau-injury-wrist-hip-back-body-pushing-back

07

PIVOT FAN-SLIDING THE POWER

A well-executed backswing generates the potential energy to power the downswing. The purpose of the downswing is to transmit the energy generated and stored in the backswing to impart as much power as possible to strike the ball.

The pivot fan-slide movement improves the efficiency of this transmission when it is deployed *throughout* the impact zone.

The Pivot Fan-slide Lubricates the Transmission.

At the top of the backswing, most of the weight of the body, 80 to 90 percent, is on the inside of the right foot and leg. The energy resides in the stretched muscles of the right side and leg, and the coiled muscles of the left upper body.

The energy stored in the stretched muscles of the entire right side/leg is ready to be released. With the left foot open to 60 - 90 degrees at the address, the stretch is also felt in the left leg. This 'stretched' sensation on both sides primes the downswing to begin reflexively.

This stretched sensation makes it instinctive to release the energy stored in the muscles of the right side/leg. It triggers an aggressive push off the ball of the right foot to initiate the downswing. A right foot, pre-turned 20 - 45* degrees toward the target, makes this push easier to execute aggressively and more efficiently. (* This push with the ball of the right foot is akin to a 100m sprinter pushing off with the ball of his right foot on the starting block. By contrast, a 'Hogan Swing' golfer pushes off with the instep - not the ball - of the square right foot; this is an inefficient movement.)

An aggressive push off the ball of the right foot as the backswing is being completed is desirable.

Once that 'push' trigger is activated, the stretched rotational muscles of the right side and the core muscles rotate the hips and lower body to transfer the body weight *onto the left heel*. The early activation of the rotational movement of the lower body at the start of the downswing *stretches* the X-Factor, resulting in more energy generated in the backswing.

The energy stored on the right side transitions seamlessly into a rotational movement of the lower body, driving and allowing the left side to *lead* the downswing.

This rotational movement of the lower body then stretches the muscles of the left side. The stretch is felt first in the left hip/thigh/leg before it gets onto the *heel* of the left foot. The left foot is opened to 60 - 90[1] degrees at the address, which encourages the rotational movement of the lower body to pivot more naturally on the *heel* of the left foot. ^

(^ Pivoting on the ball of the left foot must be avoided; it is inefficient. The other option of pivoting on the outside of the left sole is also inefficient.)

With the pivot on the left heel, the sole of the left foot opens progressively as it fan-slides *off the ground*[2] and allows the momentum of the downswing to power through. This pivot fan-slide movement[3] allows the left side to lead and dominate the downswing. It is as close to 'frictionless' as it can get; it significantly enhances the rotational power that can be delivered in a downswing.

The pivot fan-slide movement needs to be deployed progressively throughout the impact zone. This is to exploit its full potential of enhancing the rotational efficiency of the golf swing.

The pivot fan-slide movement is a trade-on mechanism that balances the requirements of power/speed and stability.

The pivot fan-slide movement[3] was demonstrated in a coaching YouTube posted in 2021: https://youtu.be/cCtFdaR5Og4 at time 0:50 to 0:56 occurring from frames 6 to 12 in the swing sequence.

The pivot fan-slide movement is also demonstrated again in the YouTube videos featured in Chapter 9.

But the first-ever instructional pivot fan-slide movement was done by Audrey Ho Mei Lian.[4]

The Push off the Ball of the Right Foot is Efficient.

The aggressive push off the ball of the right foot initiates the downswing by thrusting the body weight onto the left heel. As the left side takes charge of the swing and dominates, the right leg begins to relax and lifts off the ground. The right leg bends and follows the rotational movement of the lower body revolving on the left heel.

Throughout the downswing, the tension of the right side/leg is released continuously as the swing progresses. Hence, the right leg bends/flexes naturally and moves toward the left leg. The right leg revolves around the left leg and lands the right foot across the target line at the finish of the swing; the extent of the 'rotational follow-through' movement depends on the need for accuracy or distance of the shot.

In the first transitional move into the downswing, the left leg assumes a squat position with a bend at the knee that engages the muscles of the thigh but does not feel tense. *The left leg needs to be kept bent throughout the impact zone and beyond.* The rotational movement of the lower body is encouraged by a bent left leg with a pre-turned open left foot. ^ ^

This translates into the rotational movement of the upper body and the left side and arm, dragging the club shaft around the body/swing axis. The bent knees of both legs also define the swing path of the clubhead, which is characteristic of the golfer. ^ ^

(^ ^ In field sports, like the shot put and discus throw, both legs are bent during and after the final throw swing. Likewise, in a golf swing, both legs should be kept bent throughout the impact zone. A straightening left leg through impact is inimical to rotational movement. It reduces the distance potential of a swing and should be avoided.

The straightening of the left leg is a weak movement; the reactionary 'ground force' does not help to drive the swing. A golfer with an insufficiently open left foot needs to straighten the left leg because the left foot effectively blocks the follow-through. The rotational energy expended to overcome the 'blocking effect' of an insufficiently open left foot diminishes the distance potential of the golf swing.)

An example of a golfer who retains the bent left leg throughout the impact zone and beyond is shown here: https://youtu.be/VpFabFdA0fU occurring at time 0:42 - 0:45. Or by Gordon Sargent in: https://youtu.be/6Tv0fjK7LqU?si=uuzbZVa17Yq8Cgw4 at time 0:20.)

The Pivot Fan-slide Facilitates Rotational Movement

The key to an efficient downswing is the rotational movement of the lower body, pivoting on the left heel, and the sole of the left foot fan-sliding open *off the ground* to allow the momentum of the swing to go to a full finish.

The pivot fan-slide allows the rotational movement of the entire swing to be executed forcefully and stably, much like a spinning top revolving on its spindle. *When the rotational movement is fast enough, the right leg naturally revolves around the left leg and lands the right foot across the target line at the finish of the swing.*

This 'rotational follow-through' movement of the Convex Swing is distinctly different from the right leg being held back in the Hogan Swing's traditional follow-through. It enhances the distance potential of the Convex Swing.

This 'rotational follow-through' (right-leg-revolving-around-the-left-leg) movement is common in field sports, where the rotational movement is fully exploited to maximize the distance potential.[#]

This is something that the golf swing can imitate. The current practice of holding the right leg back in the traditional finish of a golf swing reduces the distance potential of the swing.[##]

([#] An example of the follow-through revolving movement of the legs in shot put is shown here: https://youtu.be/0Xl73JHMq34 occurring at time frames 7:35 - 7:48 minutes. In a golf swing, however, it is the right leg that crosses over the left. This video also shows the narrow stance and the bent right and left leg promoting rotational movement during the final throw from time frames 5:50 to 6:30.)

([##] Scottie Scheffler uses the pull-back of his right leg/foot to maintain the balance on his follow-through. Watch: https://youtu.

be/ubsB3Fn8AkE at time 0:35. The right foot pull-back is a trade-off action. He is better off if he lets his right leg revolve around the left leg and lands his right foot across the target line; this trade-on action will maximize his power potential.)

A forceful rotational movement can result in a right leg revolving movement to land the right foot at 270 to 360 degrees from its address position. Such a revolving movement allows the golfer to view the flight of the ball as he passes the isosceles triangle position till the right arm is at 1 o'clock to midnight and again at the completion of the follow-through.

However, in shots requiring less than a driver, like a fairway wood or a long iron, the right leg needs to revolve around the left leg and land the right foot across the target line only as much as necessary when accuracy rather than distance is utmost. The limited revolving movement can increase distance significantly without compromising the stability of the swing and the accuracy of the shot.

The pivot fan-slide allows the rotational movement of the lower body to occur within the confines of the heels. It can accommodate as much rotational power as the lower body can generate without compromising the stability of the swing. It is a key to 'frictionless' distance by design.

The Pivot Fan-slide is a Key to the Convex Strike

The pivot fan-slide movement is a unique feature, first conceived in 2020 and published in *The Reflex Convex Swing*[5].

It mimics the final movement of the hammer throw, shot put, and discus. It is a natural consequence of the very open left foot responding to the rotational movement of the lower body, pivoting on the left heel, and its sole fan-sliding *off the ground*, and needing to power through in the downswing.

This pivot on the left heel and the fan-slide of the sole *off the ground* of the left foot are two of several keys to achieving a convex bend shaft strike on the ball.

This pivot fan-slide movement confers many other attendant rotational benefits that contribute to obtaining the Convex Strike.

These other benefits are discussed in the next chapter.

(1) The combination of a pre-turned 45 degrees right foot and a 90 degrees left foot toward the target at the address was used to allow YT Siew to achieve the convex strike as detailed in Chapter 9. A golfer with a more powerful rotational speed of the lower body may require foot positions that are less oriented toward the target to achieve the convex strike.

(2) The fan-slide can open efficiently only when the sole of the left foot is *not in contact* with the ground. In other words, the body weight rotates on the left heel while the sole of the foot fans open progressively *off the ground* to accommodate the rotational movement of the lower body. The golfer feels like a spinning top revolving on its spindle.

(3) The pivot fan-slide movement is a unique amalgamation of the essential features of the rotational movement of the final swing of the hammer throw, the shot put and discus. It was devised to suit the requirements of the Convex Swing to achieve the elusive Convex Strike on the golf ball.

(4) Audrey Ho Mei Lian was the first student to be coached to play the pivot fan-slide movement. Subsequently, the author used a photo collage of that movement to help his early students visualize and understand how it can be done.

(5) The pivot fan-slide movement needs to be deployed throughout the impact zone to maximize its full distance-enhancing potential. It is to lubricate the transmission of the energy generated in the backswing into a powerful downswing force. Its distance-enhancing potential is not served if the pivot fan-slide is done *after* impact on the ball, like in Bryson DeChambeau's swing.

08

⋘⊷⟨⊙⟩⊶⋙

DELIVERING MORE ROTATIONAL BENEFITS

The rotational movement of the lower body *leads* throughout the downswing.

The 'leading' rotational movement of the lower body determines all the subsequent dependent connected downswing movements. It allows the dependent movements of the components to stay connected throughout the downswing. It dispenses with the need for conscious sequencing of its components.

This focus on the 'leading' rotational movement of the lower body makes for a truly reflexive downswing that is easier to learn.

Many desirable characteristics of a good downswing are a direct result of an increase in the rotational speed of the lower body.

An increase in rotational speed confers many benefits. These are discussed below.

Left Side Dominance

In the downswing, the right side/leg pushes off the ball of the right foot initiates the rotational movement of the lower body, which plants the body weight onto the left heel. This movement stretches the rotational muscles of the left side.

That allows the left side to lead and dominate the downswing. When that happens, many benefits accrue. And the best part is that these effects occur reflexively.

Among them are:

1. The rotational movement ensures that *the left arm remains in contact with the left chest*[1]. The left shoulder drags the left arm and club through the ball. The right arm, subconsciously responding to the dragging movement, bends and tucks its elbow progressively and naturally nearer to the right hip as the swing enters the impact zone.

2. Throughout the impact zone, *the left arm remains close to the chest.* The structure of the swing remains tight and compact, much like a figure skater entering a spin. This tight structure of the left arm remains connected to the left chest and the body as it revolves on the left heel and around the swing axis. *It improves the rotational efficiency of the swing.* The right arm merely goes along for the ride. The whole body feels like a spinning top revolving its spindle on the left heel.

3. As the left shoulder and arm drag the club through the ball, the club merely hinges on the wrists; it just responds to the rotational movement of the lower body. The dragging action allows the clubface to remain square to the swing arc. Thus, *it takes timing the impact on the ball out of the swing.*

4. The left arm behaves like the shaft of a blade of a windmill, merely revolving on the hinge. Or like that of the Iron

Byron machine. Thus, *the Convex Swing has the desirable characteristics of a 'single-plane' swing.* The swing path is determined by the body weight shifting onto the left heel and the right and left legs remaining bent throughout the impact zone. This swing plane reflects the stature of the golfer; it need not be changed to one that is shallower.

5. When the rotational movement of the lower body in a swing is the predominant source of power, the left side, shoulder, and arm dominate the downswing. There is no need to tap other sources of power, such as the release of the right arm, the rolling of the arms, and the snapping of the wrists. Such conscious movements complicate the swing, nullifying any dubious gain in power. The downswing happens too fast for such conscious actions to be executed reliably. Conscious manipulation of the arm, hands, and wrists is futile and detrimental to building a reliable repeating swing.

6. A swing that is played with the big muscles of the body and allows the left side to dominate is more consistent and less prone to succumb under pressure.

The left side dominance makes the Convex Swing more reflexive and reliable.

The left arm remains close to the chest from the top of the backswing to the isosceles triangle at 4 o'clock left arm position and to the right arm at the 2 o'clock position on the way to a full finish of the swing.

It is the rotation of the lower body that drives the left side and determines the power and the outcome of the golf shot.*

The key focus must be on increasing the speed of rotation of the lower body to retain the dominance of the left side.*

(* This emphasis on the rotational speed of the lower body does not seek to downplay the contribution of an improvement in the overall physical conditioning of the entire body. This focus is to ensure that the rotation of the lower body remains the leading movement in the downswing; this allows the left side to remain the dominant side in the downswing.)

Sequencing of Movements

When the components are connected properly in their relative orientations set at the address, it simplifies the execution of the rest of the golf swing.

The push *solely* with the left shoulder causes the backswing to move on an inclined arc to arrive at the desired CTC top of the backswing position.

At the top of the backswing, the stretched muscles of the right side and the left leg (held back by a very open left foot) make it *instinctive to initiate the downswing.*

The muscles of the right side are primed to push off the ball, rather than the instep, of the pre-turned right foot. This push triggers an aggressive rotational movement of the lower body, which plants the body weight onto the left *heel* rather than the ball of the left foot. (Pivoting on the ball of the left foot is inefficient and must be avoided.)

This aggressive first move down, as the backswing is being completed, stretches the X-Factor, thereby creating more stored energy before it is released and manifests as a powerful downswing force.

This 'leading' rotational movement of the lower body pulls everything along. The lower body rotates the upper body, which drags the left arm and club along. Because the components of the swing are connected properly in their relative orientations set at the address, they stay connected and become dependent movements responding to the rotational movement of the lower body.

Focus on the 'leading' movement of the lower body in the downswing. *All the other dependent connected movements fall sequentially in place. There is no need for any conscious thought on sequencing the dependent connected components.*

Any attempt at deliberate sequencing is futile since the downswing happens too fast (in a quarter of a second) for that to be done consciously^. It only serves to disrupt the natural, free flow of the swing.

In a reflexive connected swing, the primary focus on the rotational movement of the lower body frees *the mind from complicating sequencing thoughts.* That freedom of mind produces a free-flowing swing that is more naturally powerful.

(^ It is far better, easier, and more productive to examine the setup positions of posture and the relative orientation of the components of the swing set at the address. They influence the connectedness of a golf swing. When the components are connected properly at the address, the push *solely* with the left shoulder ensures that the components stay connected during the backswing. Then, in the downswing, the rotational movement of the lower body ensures that the dependent components stay connected to produce a free-flowing swing. This connectedness between the components dispenses with the need to sequence their movements. A detailed analysis of the cause and effect of the features mentioned can yield better solutions[2].)

Separation of the Shoulders and the Hips — the X-Factor

The separation between the shoulders and the hips is the widest at the top of the backswing. For most professional golfers, the maximum angle between the shoulder and the hip plane is about 60 degrees. *This is the maximum X-Factor attained at the top of the backswing.*

For supple golfers, an early rotation of the left hip/leg/side onto the left heel as the backswing is being completed is desirable; it increases the separation between the shoulder and hip planes. This X-Factor Stretch is key to generating more energy in the backswing.

This X-Factor Stretch is also made easier with the feet pre-turned toward the target, preferably with the right foot turned 45 degrees and the left 90 degrees. These foot positions point the hip plane left of the target line at the address. The push off the ball of the right foot is more aggressive, and the shifting of the body weight is not blocked by the very open left foot. Hence, the stretch of the X-Factor is more readily done, especially when aided by the pivot fan-slide movement on the left heel.

Beyond this initial stretch of the maximum angle occurring at the start of the downswing, it is not possible to create any more 'lag' between the shoulder and the hip planes in the downswing[3].

The aim in the rest of the downswing until impact on the ball is to *retain* as much of this shoulder/hip plane separation and as late into the downswing as possible[3]. That can be achieved by rotating the lower body as fast and for as long as possible. The wider this separation *remains*, the higher the degree of convexity of the shaft at impact on the ball.

When the separation remains sufficiently wide, the shaft does not transition from straight to a concave bend before it strikes the ball.

The shorter time and distance to impact, made possible by the Convex Swing System, enables the separation to remain sufficiently wide for the convex bend shaft to strike the ball.

The very open left foot set at the address and the pivot fan-slide deployed throughout the impact zone are also instrumental in retaining as much of the *residual* lag between the shoulder and hip planes for as long and as late into the downswing as possible.

The transmitted power in the downswing is released as a late whip-like action of the clubhead as the shaft is dragged through the ball.

Angle Between the Left Arm and the Club Shaft

In the Convex Swing, there is no need to manipulate the left wrist in the backswing.

The left arm/shaft angle is naturally obtuse at the address. When the left shoulder solely pushes the left arm and the club, *the left arm/ shaft angle stays obtuse until the top of the backswing is reached.**

(* The right arm and hand must remain passive throughout the backswing; otherwise, they can cause the left wrist to become acute at the top of the backswing. In the worst case, the right wrist can cause the shaft to point across the target line at the top of the backswing. When that happens, compensatory actions during the downswing need to be taken, making the swing less consistent.)

In the downswing, the rotational movement of the lower body is initiated by an aggressive right hip/leg/side push off the ball of the foot to shift the body weight onto the left heel.

In this first move down, the angle between the left arm and the shaft becomes acute in the downswing. The higher the speed of the rotational movement, the longer the angle remains acute, and the deeper into the impact zone, the convex bend can be retained.

The convex shape of the shaft moderates as the stored energy is released before it impacts the ball with a convex bend to a straight shaft. It takes a truly fast rotational movement of the lower body to retain a distinct convex shape in the shaft when it strikes the ball.

The primary focus must be to increase the rotational speed to retain the acute angle as far into the downswing as possible. That will allow a more convex bend to approach and impact the ball.

Swing Plane

The posture of the golfer and the relative orientations of components of the backswing are set at the address. The push of the left shoulder moves the left arm and club in an inclined arc to the top of the backswing and sets the left arm at the position of the right shoulder when viewed down the line. *This top of the backswing position and the stature of the golfer determine the backswing plane.*

In the first move down, the head dips as the body weight is shifted to the left heel, and the legs assume a more squat position. This first movement in the downswing is dictated by the rotational movement of the lower body. *This rotational movement and the squat position of the legs determine the plane of the downswing.*

When the movements of the backswing and downswing are done within the confines defined by the outer heels, the backswing and downswing axes remain stable. The swing planes of the backswing and the downswing remain essentially somewhat parallel to each other. This is as close to a single-plane swing that can be achieved.

There is no particular merit in a conscious manipulation to shallow the downswing plane. The required conscious actions, like changing the left arm and wrist orientations, detract from playing by reflex.

Strong Grip - Left 3-Knuckle Hand and Right Target-facing Palm

In the Convex Swing, the rotational movement of the lower body is the prime source of power. It allows the left side to dominate the downswing. The left side and shoulder drag the arm and club, other dependent components throughout the impact zone. The right arm merely responds to the leading left side and tucks naturally into the right hip.

The left arm does not change its orientation relative to the shoulder in a connected swing.

A strong 3-knuckle left hand grip with a target-facing right hand palm is best suited to a convex swing where the rotational movement of the lower body is the prime motive force.

It lets the left side lead and dominate the downswing while subduing the disrupting influence of the right arm.

This makes it easier to let the left shoulder drag the left side/arm/club through the impact zone without changing their relative orientations set at the address.

The left side pulls all the connected components through impact *without any need to sequence their movement.*

This allows the clubface to remain square to the swing path. *That takes timing the impact on the ball out of the swing.*

A target-facing right palm ensures that the right arm does not disrupt the free-flowing movement of the swing through impact.

Where necessary, the left hand grip can be adjusted by a half-knuckle or so to suit the golfer's speed of lower body rotation. Similarly, the right palm can be adjusted to suit.

Central Position of the Ball

When the rotational movement of the lower body is the prime motive force of the downswing, the lower body drives the upper body, and the left arm remains close to the chest. The swing revolves around the left heel, ensuring that the body and swing axes revolve within the confines of the heels.

The rotation of the lower body leads the left arm and the club throughout the impact zone. At impact on the ball, the left arm is at the 6 to 5:45 o'clock position; the left arm/shaft angle remains obtuse, and the left hand is ahead of the clubhead[4]. *The clubhead arrives in the middle of the stance; that is where the ball needs to be positioned.*

As elaborated below, the right leg needs to revolve around the left leg to allow the momentum of the downswing to follow through and land the right foot across the target line, maximizing the distance potential of the swing.

With the ball positioned in the middle of the stance, it is easier for the right leg to revolve around the left leg enhancing the rotational efficiency of the swing.

Positioning the ball forward of the center should be avoided since it requires the left arm/hand to reach out toward the ball. Conscious adjustments are necessary. This results in the left arm losing its close connection with the chest and with the rotational movement of the lower body, leading to a loss of swing speed and distance potential.

Right Leg Revolving Around the Left on Rotational Follow-Through

In the Convex Swing System, the three core principles are designed for distance, reinforcing each other as the momentum of the movements builds. The pivot fan-slide movement facilitates the rotation of the body/swing axis on the left heel.

The follow-through of the downswing momentum is facilitated by the pivot fan-slide. And it must be allowed to proceed uninterrupted.

The right leg revolves around the left leg on the follow-through momentum and lands the right foot across the target line[5]. This rotational follow-through movement helps deliver the full distance potential of the downswing.

In field sports like shot put and discus, the right leg revolves around the left leg as the implement is being released, proceeding naturally as a consequence of the continuous rotational follow-through momentum.

A golf swing needs to imitate the uninterrupted rotational follow-through movement of field sports.

This rotational movement, where the right leg revolves around the left leg on follow-through, capitalizes on the continuous momentum of the downswing, optimizing performance.

In the Hogan Swing, the right leg/foot is often held back to maintain stability in the follow-through. However, this trade-off movement reduces the distance potential of a Hogan Swing.

The above-mentioned rotational benefits supplement those described in the last five Chapters 3 to 7. Together, they contribute to achieving the elusive Convex Strike on the ball.

The elusive feat of a Convex Strike on the ball is waiting to happen in the next chapter.

(1) The greater the rotational speed of the lower body, the longer the left arm remains close to the left chest throughout the impact zone.

This focus on the rotational speed of the lower body is the key to power in a downswing. Crucially important to obtain the Convex Strike on the ball.

The phenomenon of the left arm staying close to the chest is best demonstrated by the kid in the red shirt, named Conner, in https://youtu.be/wuZVSwXKLjs?si=lVAsmZC8VzZIZGkB. View the time segment 2:04 to 2:14. The left arm stays with the left chest from the top of the backswing, throughout the impact zone, and past impact till the left arm is at 4 o'clock position.

YT Siew copied the unique ability of Conner, the kid in the red shirt, to keep his left arm close to the chest as a model to refine his swing. It contributed to his effort in achieving the Convex Strike on the ball. Details are in Chapter 9.

(2) To develop a connected swing, it is important to adopt a posture where the components of the swing are connected in their natural or preset orientations to each other. It determines the obtuse left arm and shaft angle set at the address. When that is done, the push *solely* with the left shoulder in executing the backswing ensures that the components stay connected. Details on posture, stance, ball position, setup, etc, are described in Chapter 6 of *The Reflex Convex Swing.*

In the downswing, the push off the ball of the right foot initiates the 'leading' rotational movement of the lower body, which drags the dependent connected components along, thereby retaining the connectedness of the swing. That does away with any need to sequence their movements.

(3) One aim of the downswing has been often stated erroneously, as creating 'lag' between the lower body and the upper body. This 'lag' is a misnomer as it gives it a wrong connotation that the upper body and left arm are held back deliberately in the downswing.

The separation between the shoulder and hip planes is at a maximum at the top of the backswing. In the first move down, the push off the ball of the right foot, as the backswing is being completed, initiates the rotational movement of the lower body to plant the body weight onto the left heel. These early movements serve to stretch the X-Factor. This X-Factor Stretch is the only time when the 'lag' between the shoulder and hip plane has increased.

Beyond this initial stretch, more lag cannot be 'created' in the downswing. The aim must be to *retain* as much as possible the extent of what remains of the 'lag', not to create it. The only way to retain that is to rotate the lower body as fast as possible and not by holding back the upper body.

(4) In the Convex Swing System, the left arm travels two '10-minute' clock face movements from the top of the backswing to a 6 to 5.45 o'clock position to impact the ball. During that time, the shaft of the club reaches its maximum convexity and straightens to impact the ball. At that point (6 to 5.45 o'clock position), the left arm and hand are ahead of the clubhead. A ball placed at the center of the stance reduces the chance of the shaft transitioning to a concave bend before impact on the ball.

(5) In field sports, like the shot put and discus, it is imperative for the thrower's right leg to revolve around the left leg on follow-through momentum before and as the implement is being released. And the rotation of the body continues for a few more times. This is needed to maximize distance.

The golf swing needs to adopt the 'right-leg-revolving-around-the-left-leg' rotational follow-through movement. This movement on follow-through lands the right foot across the target line by about 90 degrees for shots needing accuracy and by 180 degrees for drives where the intent is maximum distance.

When that happens, the right foot lands 270 to 360 degrees from its address position. Throughout the follow-through, it is eminently possible for the golfer to track the flight of the ball from the isosceles triangle position till the right arm reaches the 1 o'clock to midnight position.

09

ACHIEVING THE ULTIMATE GRAIL OF GOLF

The concepts advanced in the Convex Swing System have increased the rotational efficiency of the golf swing. Consequently, they have reduced the threshold rotational speed of the lower body to achieve the convex strike on the ball.

That notwithstanding, YT Siew worked diligently to strengthen his body in two areas crucial to obtaining the convex strike. Those exercises are described in Chapter 3 of this book. He has also employed other exercises to achieve the desired objective.

After acquiring the needed strength, YT was able to execute the Convex Swing efficiently. He was able to tap into the benefits offered by the many enabling features of the Convex Swing System elaborated upon in Chapters 4 to 8.

Right Foot pre-turned 45 degrees toward the target

His supple body required that the right foot at the address be pre-turned 45 degrees toward the target to hold his right hip/thigh/side sufficiently sturdy in the backswing. This allowed the full strength of his left shoulder, arm and side to push firmly against the right hip/leg. Over time, the push of the left shoulder and the resistance of the right hip/leg interactively strengthened each other. This generated the maximum energy in a compact backswing. The X-Factor of 60 degrees between the shoulder and hip planes was also achieved at the top of the backswing.

With the right foot pre-turned 45 degrees, the left arm at the top of the backswing was at the 10 o'clock position.

The shorter backswing allowed the left arm to move over a shorter route to impact the ball in the shortest time possible. The left arm needed to travel a clock-face 20-minutes to impact the ball while that of the Hogan Swing required 30-minutes. That represented a one-third reduction of the rotational distance/time to impact. For details, refer to Chapter 5.

The shorter route and time allowed the downswing force to *retain* the convex bend shaft as far into the impact zone as possible.

The rotational exercises prepared his body to execute the downswing with the required speed. In the downswing, the right foot pre-turned 45 degrees was also better positioned to push off the ball of the right foot. The aggressive push off the ball of the right foot set in motion the rotational movement of the lower body. The resultant rotational thrust of the left hip/thigh shifted faster and more body weight onto the left heel. This effectively stretched the X-Factor, thereby creating more energy to power the downswing.

The enhanced acceleration of the rotation of the lower body drove the left side, engaged the pivot fan-slide earlier, and revolved the entire body on the left heel and around the swing axis. The leading movement of the lower body driving the left side throughout the downswing has characterized the convex swing as a left side dominant swing, much like the hammer throw in field sports.[1]

Left Foot pre-turned towards the target

The left foot at the address was pre-turned towards the target 90 degrees. This made it easier to land the body weight on the left heel and deploy the fan-slide movement earlier in the downswing. The left foot fan-slid its sole *just off the ground* while pivoting on its heel; this reduced the resistance to the rotational movement of the lower body. Hence, this virtually 'frictionless' pivot fan-slide movement has lubricated the transmission of the energy generated in the backswing to power the downswing.

The very open left foot and the pivot fan-slide have effectively diminished substantially the resistance provided by the left leg/side in impeding the rotational movement of the lower body in the downswing. ***This mimics the unique feature of the Iron Byron, a club-testing machine, having only an arm without a 'left leg' blocking the through swing.*** And that feature largely accounted for the Iron Byron unique ability to do the convex strike on the ball.

With the body weight on the left heel, the swing behaved like a spinning top revolving very stably on its spindle. The accelerating momentum of the downswing caused the right leg to revolve around the left leg on an aggressive rotational follow-through* - a common feature in field sports like the shot put and discus throw.

(* This is a stark contrast to many professional golfers using the Hogan Swing trying to hold back the right leg to maintain balance in the follow-through, thereby sacrificing some distance potential in their swings.)

With such a powerful rotational movement, the right foot moved from the address position, revolved around the left leg and landed across the target line, typically by about 240 - 270 degrees. That allowed him to view the flight of the ball after it had been struck. When needed as in a driver swing, the right foot can land at the finish at approximately its starting position which is a 360 degrees rotation.

More Benefits from the 45/90 degrees Feet Positions

With the right foot pre-turned 45 degrees and the left 90 degrees toward the target set at the address, the hip line pointed left of the target line.

During the backswing, pushing *solely* with the left shoulder allowed the left arm and club to move inside the hip line and consequently, more along the target line. That way the right knee could be kept sturdy. (Moving the left arm and club too much inside the target line can destabilize the right knee.)

During the backswing, the left shoulder push retained the obtuse left-arm/shaft angle assumed at the address until the top of the backswing was reached; *this kept the swing arc wide without the left arm disconnecting from the left chest.* A strong left shoulder allowed the left arm to remain relatively tension free and straight and the right arm passive. (Maintaining the obtuse left-arm/shaft angle during the backswing is a notable feature of the Cameron Young swing.)

With the pre-turned hip plane at the address of 30 degrees left of the target line (as a result of the 45/90 feet positions), the rotational movement of the lower body had a jump-start in the downswing, thus making the rotation more efficient in the downswing.

The pre-turned hip plane allowed the left shoulder to push the left arm and shaft more along the target line. Consequently, the downswing plane stayed more aligned (or 'parallel') to the target line, allowing for a potentially more consistently straight shot.

Benefits from a Better Head and Shoulder Plane Tilt

The pre-turned hip plane encouraged the left shoulder to move along the target line and upward on an inclined arc during the backswing. It also allowed the shoulder plane a more upright tilt that is more aligned to the downswing plane. The head-neck axis rotated in sync with the shoulder tilt.

By responding to the rotational movement of the lower body, the steeper shoulder tilt allowed the left arm to stay closer to the chest and the right elbow closer to the right hip as it moved into impact position. This tighter structure promoted the rotational efficiency of the swing.

The shaft maintained a more convex bend closer to impact on the ball - thereby achieving the convex strike on the ball.

Those changes also allowed the isosceles triangle to occur higher on followthrough - sign of an efficient swing.

YT's Convex Strike has been posted on YouTube

YT's diligent effort over time produced a swing that struck the ball with a straight shaft. The shaft has a distinct convex bend in the first movement down which transitions into a straight shaft *without going through the concave bend before impacting the ball.*

YT's swing has produced a Convex Strike on the ball.

YT's swing sequences were posted on YouTube: https://www.youtube.com/watch?v=B1n4_AWcxlY on June 28th 2024. The YouTube videos featured the Driver and 5 Wood swings.

Scan QR code with your smartphone to watch the YT's Convex Strike will transform the Game of Golf.

(The YouTube videos were taken with a Samsung S20 phone. The camera function was set to Video, Super Slo-Mo mode. This mode captured the videos in slow motion up to 960 frames per second in 720p resolution.)

In the downswing, the shaft had a convex bend early, then transitioned to a slight convex bend to straight when the left arm was at 8 and 7 o'clock position, and remained straight before it struck the ball with a straight shaft at impact. (But the shaft did not transition to a concave bend before it struck the ball.)

The apparent straight shaft just before, and at impact was probably a slight convex bend because the rolling shutter effect served to make the bend look less convex.[2]

Those swings, recorded in slow motion mode, proved beyond reasonable doubt that YT has achieved the unprecedented Convex Strike* on the ball.

(* A convex strike is taken as one that impacts the ball with an 'apparent' straight shaft made less convex by the rolling shutter effect. At no time does the shaft assume a concave bend throughout the impact zone before impact on the ball. It would take a truly high rotational speed of the lower body to impact the ball with a visibly obvious convex bend shaft. The higher rotational speed required to do the 'pure' convex strike naturally produces the attendant greater distance expected of a convex strike. That can likely be done by most professional golfers as discussed in Chapter 10.)

The YT swings showed that it was eminently possible to strike the ball with a convex bend shaft - a feat previously thought not possible. YT's effort corroborated the convex strike first achieved by the Iron Byron, a club-testing machine, as elaborated upon in Epilogue (1).

The Convex Strike as captured on Screenshots

The Convex Strikes of the Driver and Fairway Wood are reproduced here as collages of screenshots taken from the videos used in the YouTube posted on June 28th 2024: https://photos. app.goo.gl/z1dqgbNcVMST4jse7 and https://photos.app.goo.gl/ NALuhvyuwcD5tRay7

Scan QR code with your smartphone to watch the YT's Convex Strike using a driver.

Scan QR code with your smartphone to watch the YT's Convex Strike using a 5-wood.

Fig 9.1 A Convex Strike using a Driver

Backswing

Downswing

Rotational Follow-through

Fig 9.2 A Convex Strike using a 5 Wood

Backswing

Downswing

Rotational Follow-through

Figures 9.1 and 9.2 show the notable positions of the Convex Swing using the Driver and 5 Wood.

The screenshot sequences show that the convex shape of the shaft at the left arm's 8 o'clock position changes to straight at impact 6:15 o'clock. It does not change to concave shape before it strikes the ball. ^ (^ This distinguishes the Convex Swing from the invariable transition to a concave bend shaft of the Hogan Swing before it strikes the ball.)

The screenshots show the Convex Swing deploying a convex bend shaft from the top of the swing to straight throughout the impact zone and strike the ball with a straight shaft at impact.[2]

Post impact, the shaft reverts to convex, then straight and finally concave.

YT has become the first golfer to accomplish the Convex Strike on the ball - the grail of golf previously considered impossible.

(Figure 9.3 shows YT using the 7 Iron to do the Convex Strike: https://photos.app.goo.gl/c1p7j4o6qaFdbfMc7. The 7 Iron swing can have a less full rotational follow-through when accuracy takes precedence over distance.)

Scan QR code with your smartphone to watch the YT's Convex Strike using a 7-iron.

Fig 9.3 A Convex Strike using a 7 Iron

Backswing

Downswing

Rotational Follow-through

YT's Convex Swing is Efficient

At the address, his 'armpit-width' stance is narrow, his right foot is turned 45 degrees toward the target and his left 90.

Due to regular practice, his body is supple. Hence, he needs to have his right foot pre-turned at 45 degrees in order to arrive at the top of his backswing with the left arm at the 10 o'clock position. This short compact backswing does not compromise the generation of energy since his shoulders are turned fully against the hips held sturdy by the right foot/leg. It achieves the desired X-Factor of 60 degrees, advocated by Ben Hogan.

He adopts a 90 degrees left foot at the address to make it easier to transfer the body weight onto the left heel, pivots on it, and allows the sole of the left foot to fan-slide *just off the ground* while its left heel remains on the ground. This enables the pivot fan-slide to be deployed early in the impact zone. The pivot fan-slide allows the left leg to stay bent longer throughout the impact zone. A bent left leg promotes rotational movement. Thus, the full potential of the downswing force is exploited via the fan-slide movement *throughout the impact zone.*

The 90 degrees left foot and the attendant pivot fan-slide promotes the *anti-clockwise* rotational movement of the lower body in the downswing. It is close to not having a left leg blocking the momentum of the downswing; that mimics the Iron Byron machine which does not have a left side to block its follow-through.

YT's swing has the hallmarks of a good swing that can stand critical examination. Namely,

1. In executing the backswing, the left shoulder solely pushes the left arm and club on an inclined arc with the neck as

center. This push solely with the left shoulder maintains the *connectedness* of the components in a backswing. Thus this push maintains the relative position of the connected components throughout the backswing.

2. More importantly, the push *solely* with the left shoulder ensures that the right arm is passive during the entire backswing and during the first movement of the downswing. It minimizes the instinctive and disruptive influence of the dominant right arm in a golf swing.

3. The sole use of the left shoulder allows the obtuse arm/shaft angle assumed at the address to *remain* obtuse until the top of the backswing is reached. The backswing arc is kept naturally wide with the left arm remaining close and connected to the chest. The shaft is naturally pointed skyward, left of the target line and above horizontal. When viewed down-the-line, the left arm at the top of the backswing covers the right shoulder; this validates the push *solely* with the left shoulder has maintained the *connectedness* of the components of the backswing and resulted in a swing plane that is not too upright or flat.

4. A compact and stable backswing with the left shoulder pushed fully against a sturdy right foot/side generates the maximum energy in the backswing. This is the X-Factor of about 60 degrees between the shoulder and hip planes at the top of the backswing.

5. An aggressive push off the ball of the right foot initiates the rotation of the lower body and encourages the left hip to revolve around the swing axis, thereby stretching the X-Factor. That contributes to generating more energy as the backswing is completed.

6. An aggressive push off the ball of the right foot allows the rotational movement of the lower body to 'lead' the downswing. This ensures that the left arm stays close to the chest for as long into the downswing as possible. This tight structure of the upper body improves the rotational efficiency of the swing.

7. This 'leading' rotational movement of the lower body determines the movement of the connected components in the downswing. It drags the left shoulder, arm and club through the impact zone. That connectedness of the dependent components dispenses with the need to sequence their movements. It also takes the timing out of the swing. They make the swing more reflexive and repeatable.

8. The aggressive first movement down causes the left arm/shaft angle to become acute and remains so further into the impact zone. This contributes to a convex strike.

9. A left leg that is kept bent throughout the impact zone allows the rotational movement of the lower body to keep accelerating through, until and past impact. A bent left leg allows the downswing to be more aligned (or parallel) to the backswing plane.

10. A pivot fan-slide movement is deployed *throughout the impact zone* to deliver as much power as is available in a downswing. The pivot fan-slide makes the downswing feel 'frictionless'. (The open left foot and the pivot fan-slide dispenses with the need to straighten the left leg or even lifting it off the ground as evident in many professional golfer swings. A straightening left leg is inimical to rotational speed. This very open left foot and pivot fan-slide movement is a key

feature that differentiates YT's convex swing and makes it more efficient.)

11. At impact, the left arm stays close to the chest with a nice shoulder tilt, a result of the left side leading the downswing. *With the ball at the middle of the stance, the left arm does not need to leave the left chest to reach the ball, thereby retaining connectedness and enhancing the swing's distance potential.*

12. Past impact, the shaft assumes a convex bend before it straightens again.

13. An isosceles triangle formed by the arms and the shoulders occurs well into the follow-through, an indicator of an efficient swing.

14. In the rotational follow-through, the pivot fan-slide allows the swing axis to rotate on the left heel; the right leg revolves around the left leg and lands the right foot across the target line. At the finish of a driver swing, the right foot can land itself about 360 degrees from its address position. For a fairway wood or an iron shot, the right foot lands about 45 - 90 degrees across the target line or 225 - 270 degrees from the address position, without compromising the accuracy and stability of the shot.

The Convex Strike is now a Reality

The probability of a convex strike was conceived in 2019 and published in *The Reflex Convex Swing*. Now that it has been done, the 'impossible' is no more. It does not seem that difficult after all.

The three mutually reinforcing core principles, the innovative pivot fan-slide movement and the attendant enabling features of the Convex Swing System make the convex strike easier to achieve. Hence they open the way for an amateur golfer like YT to accomplish it.

The Convex Swing System provides the platform to achieve the Convex Strike. It will revolutionize the game of golf.

Not only that, golf will appeal to a wider audience because the Convex Swing is easier to learn and play with. Golf will be more fun. (More on this is in Epilogue 2.)

Given that an amateur like YT Siew has achieved the 'impossible', there is no doubt professional golfers can use the Convex Swing System to achieve the Convex Strike on the ball.

To professional golfers, the Convex Swing System holds the promise of unprecedented distance off the tee and transforming the game. The Convex Strike is the key to ultimate distance.

The next chapter discusses the direction in which professional golfers can exploit the potential possibilities that the Convex Swing System can offer.

[1] The convex swing is a left side dominant swing where the focus is to maintain the left arm as close to the left chest as long as possible into the impact zone and past impact. This aspect of the left arm being close to the left chest and the head and shoulder tilt is modeled on the swing of Conner, the kid in the red shirt, in the video: https://youtu.be/wuZVSwXKLjs. This feature is displayed, to a lesser extent, by Ariya Jutanugarn: https://youtu.be/3wru0WH0buk.

[2] The 'rolling shutter effect' phenomenon makes the convexity of a convex bend shaft throughout the impact zone appear less so than

it actually is. Thus, a convex strike occurs when the shaft transitions from convex bend to straight and remains straight before striking the ball with an 'apparent' straight shaft. At no time during the downswing does the shaft assume a concave bend.

10

TRANSFORMING THE GAME

At the time of writing *The Reflex Convex Swing* and this book, all professional golfers that I have watched on YouTube and TV approach and strike the ball with a *concave* bend shaft.

The 'concave strikes' at the impact of the best and longest driving professionals, are shown in the YouTubes at the times indicated in numerals: Bryson DeChambeau https://youtu.be/Q638_mBhYmE 2:20, Jon Rahm https://youtu.be/KN837Eda6rM 1:25, Tiger Woods https://youtu.be/Jlp8G9paliw 0:16, Rory McIlroy https://youtu.be/nhk6mAGZpOg?si=Sat9hNH6Y2tIzIk9 0:54, Cameron Young https://youtu.be/BmkSidD0Qmg 0:34, Lexi Thompson https://youtu.be/yqaWP4S0r2c 1:05, 1:19, Ariya Jutanugarn 3 wood https://youtu.be/3wru0WH0buk 1:13, Patty Tavatanakit https://youtu.be/GZyvydRF03A 1:53, Sung-Hyun Park https://youtu.be/jdsyOy3mx2o 1:50. Lilia Vu https://youtu.be/9GL3THXjIas?si=OticrH1uxka2kyii 1:30 and Ruoning Yin https://youtu.be/rHEkDHZSGOE?si=ktRh4ruSohTgte5G 1:09.

They all approach the ball with a *concave* bend shaft before impacting the ball.* No matter how strong they are. And no matter how powerful their swings are!

(* Even the latest long-hitting golf sensations, Gordon Sargent and Christo Lamprecht, strike the ball with a concave bend shaft at impact https://youtu.be/6Tv0fjK7LqU?si=nOKX5wOpjTJApyjV 0:30 and - https://youtu.be/4ju75Ug-elg?si=TZi_5a-d_8wkmdep 0:07.)

During the downswing, the shafts of the clubs in the YouTube videos mentioned above transitioned from convex to straight from the top of the backswing to the left arm at the 7 or 8 o'clock position, a clock face movement time of 20 minutes or less. Thereafter, the shafts invariably became concave before they struck the ball at impact.

But those outcomes can be readily changed.

All those professionals have the necessary strength in the rotational muscles of their lower body to do that.

They need to deploy the power in those muscles efficiently.

All of them can achieve the Convex Strike on the ball.**

(** The Convex Strike entails that the shaft transitions from a convex bend throughout the impact zone to be at least straight at impact; it is straight at impact because the rolling shutter effect of the camera makes a convex bend shaft appear less so. But the shaft does not transition to a concave bend before it strikes the ball.)

How can professional golfers achieve the Convex Strike?

They need to adopt all three core principles of the Convex Swing System or at least two of them.

They need to:

1. Use the narrow 'armpit-width' stance at the address,

2. Pre-turn at the address the right foot 20 - 45 degrees and the left 60 - 90 degrees toward the target, and then

3. Rotate the body weight onto the *heel*, and not the ball, of the left foot in the first move downswing so as to perform the pivot fan-slide automatically.

To a professional golfer, doing a Convex Strike on the ball using the Convex Swing System is like a gimme![1] (The falsifiability of this claim can be readily tested by any professional golfer. Just do the Karl Popper Test. A debate on this matter is best settled that way[1].)

The Convex Strike will be a common occurrence. It is like the '4-minute mile' of golf. Once it is done, more and more professional golfers will be able to do it sooner rather than later.

The relentless pursuit of ever-increasing distance will ensure that all three elements of the Convex Swing System feature prominently in the professional game.

In fact, amateur golfers with sufficient speed in the rotational movement of the lower body can achieve the Convex Strike on the ball too.

The three core principles of the Convex Swing System are the keys to enhanced distances for all golfers, irrespective of whether the Convex Strike is within their reach.

The Convex Swing System: A Platform for Success

The Reflex Convex Swing provides the platform to facilitate the Convex Strike on the ball. Its three core principles are:

1. At the address, use a narrow 'armpit-width' stance.

2. At the address, pre-turn the right foot to 20 to 45 degrees and the left foot 60 to 90 degrees toward the target.

3. In the downswing, rotate the lower body to transfer the body weight onto the left heel, pivot, and revolve around the swing axis on it, and allow the left foot sole fan-slide open naturally to accommodate the swing momentum throughout the impact zone to a full finish. The rotational movement of the lower body causes the right leg to revolve around the left leg and land the right foot across the target line on rotational follow-through momentum.

The principles of the Convex Swing System are geared toward increasing the rotational efficiency of the golf swing.

All the features of the Convex Swing System mutually reinforce each other, accentuating the *anti-clockwise* movement of the downswing. These features are designed for distance!

The Convex Swing is more efficient than the Ben Hogan Swing on seven counts:

1. The rotational movement of the lower body of the Convex Swing is more powerful than the Hogan Swing 'slide and turn' movement.[2]

2. The narrow 'armpit-width' stance[3] allows the rotational movement of the lower body to be much more efficient without compromising the stability of the swing.

3. The pre-turned right foot toward the target 20 - 45 degrees[4] holds the right hip/leg more sturdy during the backswing, making the generation of energy in the backswing more efficient.

4. The pre-turned right foot encourages the use of the ball of the foot, rather than the instep, to initiate a more aggressive move to start the downswing as the backswing is being

completed. The resultant X-Factor Stretch increases the energy available to power the downswing.

5. The left foot pre-turned toward the target 60 - 90 degrees[4] enables the rotational movement of the lower body in the downswing to drive through *unrestricted*. The very open left foot does not block the momentum of the downswing movement. (By contrast, the '22 degrees' left foot of the Hogan Swing effectively blocks the momentum of the downswing.)

6. The anti-clockwise rotational movement of the downswing pivots on the left heel, allowing the left sole to fan-slide just *off the ground* as the downswing progresses. It is this pivot and fan-slide movement that allows the swing to occur stably within the confines of heels. This 'frictionless' movement enhances the rotational mechanical efficiency of the swing. The pivot fan-slide mechanism is the trade-on facility that balances the requirements of power/speed and stability in a swing.

7. The lower body rotates, pivots, and fan-slides on the left heel to allow the right leg to revolve around the left leg on follow-through momentum and land the right foot across the target line. It is a trade-on technique imported from field sports that allows a full follow-through momentum of the downswing. This rotational follow-through movement maximizes the distance potential of the downswing.

For those reasons, the Convex Swing is able to deliver a convex bend shaft to impact the ball. They also explain why the Hogan Swing has not achieved the Convex Strike on the ball (and probably unlikely to do so).

The rotational movement of the lower body over a narrow 'armpit-width' stance has a distinct advantage over the 'slide and turn' movement over a wide 'shoulder-width' stance.

For example, when the shot put (a field sport) changed to use the 'spin or rotation' technique in place of the traditional 'slide and turn', it transformed the game. Seventeen of the 25 longest all-time throws used the 'spin or rotation' technique[2]. The average distance of the 'rotation' throws was 20 percent further.

So, it should not be a surprise that the Convex Swing's Convex Strike Force (CSF) can deliver at least 20 percent more distance. That would be phenomenal compared to the meager 5 percent increase in driving distance over the last two decades.[5]

The Convex Swing Looks Distinctly Different

The 'new' Convex Swing radically alters how a golf swing looks, especially to those who are familiar only with the Hogan Swing. It looks distinctly different in many aspects.

The 'armpit-width' stance is significantly narrower but is wide enough to promote the rotational movement of the lower body while maintaining stability#. It makes it easier for the body weight to transfer to and rotate on the left heel.

(# The stance of the final throw is narrow in field sports like the hammer throw, discus, and shot put. But it is wide enough to ensure that the final throw is stable and does not compromise the distance potential available in those field sports.)

The feet are radically oriented toward the target to facilitate the anti-clockwise movement of the downswing. The momentum of the downswing naturally causes the body weight to pivot on the left heel and fan-slide the sole *off the ground;* the resultant near 'frictionless' movement improves the rotational efficiency of the lower body. It is this pivot fan-slide movement that allows the powerful rotational movement of the swing to occur stably within the confines of the heels.

The enhanced rotational movement of the lower body requires the right leg to revolve around the left leg on follow-through momentum and land the right foot across the target line##. In the future, more golfers will probably 'spin' as a shot putter or a discus thrower does on rotational follow-through momentum. The pivot fan-slide movement allows the swing to maintain its balance on follow-through.

(## A professional golfer, playing with the Hogan Swing, uses the right leg to maintain balance by holding it back or even sliding it back. This trade-off restricted follow-through movement compromises its distance potential. A prime example is Scottie Scheffler holding his right foot back: https://youtu.be/ubsB3Fn8AkE?si=4-Qz1ELcTsMYQSRg time 0:36.

The Convex Swing encourages the right leg to revolve around the left leg and land the foot across the target line to trade-on the rotational follow-through momentum to maximize its distance potential.)

A professional golfer may not need to deploy the full extent of the available rotational movement to achieve the Convex Strike. But to maximize distance, a rotational follow-through momentum that lands the right foot across the target line and closer to 360 degrees from its address position can be helpful, perhaps even desirable.

When a new swing arrives, it transforms the way it is viewed. Like the Fosbury Flop changed the high jump. Or the 'spin' technique changed the shot put. So, the Convex Swing may look strange until it is commonplace.

The Convex Strike is the Ultimate Arbiter of Distance

As it stands now, professional golfers using the Hogan Swing have displayed a convex bend shaft at the 7 to 8 o'clock left arm position in the downswing. But the shaft invariably straightens after that and transitions to a concave bend before it strikes the ball.

By adopting the core principles of the Convex Swing System, all professional golfers can use the Convex Swing to achieve the Convex Strike and exploit its ultimate distance potential. They can do that in a number of ways.

First, the right foot can be used to control the length of the backswing and the amount of rotational time to impact on the ball. This, in turn, can determine the ultimate distance potential of the golf swing.

By turning the right foot 45 degrees^ toward the target at the address, the left arm can be taken to the 9 o'clock top of the backswing position. From there, the left arm needs only a 15-minute clock face movement to impact at 6 o'clock^ with a convex bend shaft.

A professional golfer can also use a 30-degree^ pre-turned right foot to have a left arm at 10 o'clock^ at the top of the backswing position. From there, his left arm needs to travel 20 minutes to impact at 6 o'clock with a convex bend shaft.

Similarly, a professional golfer using a 20-degree^ pre-turned right foot can have a left arm at the 11 o'clock^ top of the backswing position; the left arm needs to travel 25 minutes to impact.

Ultimately, a professional golfer using a 10-degree pre-turned right foot can have a left arm at the 12 o'clock ^ top of the backswing position; the left arm needs to travel 30 minutes to impact.

(^ The amount that the right foot is pre-turned, the left arm position attained at the top of the backswing, and the time required to impact are probable estimates. They vary with the suppleness and strength of the individual golfer concerned.)

A longer backswing can deliver greater distance provided the convex bend can be retained in the downswing.

The above 'thought' experiments postulate that the distance off the tee can be maximized reliably by using the right foot to control the length of the backswing. But a longer backswing needs to be matched by a high enough rotational speed of the lower body to deliver a convex bend shaft to strike the ball at impact.

Second, a pre-turned left foot 60 - 90 degrees at the address makes it easier to transfer the body weight onto the left heel. For the supple golfer, a 90-degree left foot is preferred.

At the address, the hip line is already pointing left of the target line. With this 'advance' starting position, the rotational movement of the lower body can take the upper body more easily around the swing axis on the downswing.

As the backswing is completed, the first move in the downswing is encouraged by the push off the ball of the pre-turned right foot and the ensuing rotation of the lower body is not blocked by the very open left foot. Thus, it becomes easier to stretch the X-Factor as the backswing is completed.

The very open left foot also encourages the body weight to revolve around the swing axis. This rotation of the entire body on the left heel is not inhibited and occurs more readily throughout the impact zone.

These two effects maximize the distance potential that can be obtained from a golf swing.

Third, the resultant pivot fan-slide is virtually a 'frictionless' movement that enhances the efficiency of the rotational movement of the lower body.

The pivot fan-slide movement facilitates two finishes on follow-through:

1. The right leg revolves around the left leg on a limited follow-through momentum,[6]

2. The whole body rotates on the left heel and lands the right foot at its address position; this is a 360-degree revolution of the right leg/hip from its address position, around the target line and finishes near its initial address position.

The first limited follow-through is preferred when accuracy is a priority. The second complete follow-through may be used to maximize distance off the tee.

The pivot fan-slide allows the rotational movement to be done stably with the right leg revolving around the left leg on rotational follow-through momentum and landing the right foot across the target line.

Fourth, the rotational movement of the lower body, pivoting on the left heel to allow the right leg to revolve around the left leg, has been widely adopted in field sports; notably the shot put and discus. Why not golf?

The Convex Swing System provides the means to the Convex Strike.

The Convex Strike is the ultimate arbiter of distance.

Any Professional Golfer can do the Convex Strike (The Grail of Golf)

The possibilities considered in the preceding sections can tap into previously unknown sources of power.

Bryson DeChambeau ignited a recent journey in search of unprecedented distance for many more to follow. Who knows how far a professional golfer can take the Convex Swing?

The Convex Swing System provides the platform to the desired and ultimate Convex Strike on the ball.

Now, any professional golfer can use it to achieve the Convex Strike (The Grail of Golf). And the Convex Strike Force (CSF) can propel the ball further by perhaps 20%.

The Convex Strike is here to stay.

The convex bend of the shaft is stronger than the concave bend to strike the ball.

The convex bend is here to stay because there is no third way.

The Convex Strike on the ball is truly disruptive.

It will change the game.

Can the Convex Swing supplant the Hogan Swing?

The Convex Swing System is, thus far, the only platform to obtain the Convex Strike - the ultimate Grail of Golf.

Will the Convex Swing supplant the Hogan Swing? Eventually? Only time will tell.

The Hogan Swing's wide 'shoulder-width' stance is not conducive to rotational movement. It requires a 'slide and turn' movement to transfer the body weight to the left side. By contrast, the narrow 'armpit-width' of the Convex Swing promotes rotational movement.

In shot put (a field sport), the 'spin' technique has replaced the 'slide and turn'.

Going by that development, the rotational movement of the lower body over a narrow stance of the Convex Swing can prevail.

In addition, the Hogan Swing has an insufficiently open left foot, at 22 degrees turned toward the target. That left foot/leg effectively blocks the momentum of the anti-clockwise rotational movement of the lower body in the downswing[7].

These two 'momentum-impeding' features of the Hogan Swing cannot stand unresolved.

These 'momentum' blocks need to be removed for the golf swing technique to develop further.

The Convex Swing System has redressed the three major shortcomings of the Ben Hogan Swing.

Once the mental blocks are removed, more professional golfers will opt to emulate the rotational follow-through of field sports. They will adopt 'the right leg revolving around the left leg and landing the right foot across the target line' movement, which allows the downswing momentum to proceed naturally and continue unabated to a full finish.

It would seem likely that the Convex Swing can supplant the Hogan Swing.

Does the Convex Swing have a fighting chance?

Probably. Because the Convex Swing System has already achieved the Convex Strike on the golf ball. It was used by YT Siew, an amateur who learned it from scratch.

YT is the first human golfer to have emulated the Convex Strike done by Iron Byron, a club-testing machine[7] (Epilogue 1 has the details). YT's corroborative achievement is significant.

The Convex Strike is no longer a figment of the imagination!

A golfer, professional or recreational, with the requisite rotational speed of the lower body, can achieve the Convex Strike. He only needs to adopt the narrow 'armpit-width' stance and the pre-turned positions of the right and left feet of the Convex Swing System. And those are simple changes.

The Convex Swing System is the only platform, thus far, to achieve the Convex Strike.

Any professional golfer can use the Convex Swing System to achieve the Convex Strike. *Every professional golfer can emulate the 'pure' Convex Strike done by Iron Byron.*[1]

Since the Convex Swing is easy to learn and play with, it can be widely adopted.

But will it be? Only time will tell.

Since the Convex Strike is the ultimate arbiter of distance, and the Convex Swing System is the only platform, thus far, to achieve it, hope springs eternal!

Without hope, what is the point of dreaming?

I have a dream: A professional golfer or two will have the audacity to do the Karl Popper Test and achieve the Convex Strike. And use it to win a Tour event or two.

Indeed, who can resist the seductive allure of the Convex Strike as the ultimate route to greater distance?

Then, the Convex Strike will truly begin to transform the Game.

[1] The falsifiability of this claim can be readily tested by any professional golfer. There is no need for a lengthy debate on this claim. The Karl Popper Test was proposed in his book The Logic of Scientific Discovery (1934).

The professional golfer needs to adopt all three principles of the Convex Swing System. The swing will result in a convex bend shaft approaching and then striking the ball with a straight shaft. The shaft will not transition to a concave bend before it strikes the ball.

Indeed, the professional will be able to retain the convex bend shaft and drag it through impact on the ball and replicate the 'pure' Convex Strike done by Iron Byron. The 'pure' Convex Strike will be commonplace in the professional game.

[2] https://en.wikipedia.org/wiki/Shot_put. 17 of the longest 25-shot puts used the 'spin' technique. The average distance of the spin throws was 20 percent longer. Thus, the rotational movement of the lower body can similarly propel the ball further than the 'slide and turn' movement.

[3] The 'Convex Swing' stance may be referred to as the 'armpit-width' stance. It is where the distance between the inner heels is the same as that between the armpits. This is also the same as the distance

between the outer edges of the heels and those of the shoulders; this may be referred to as the 'new' shoulder-width stance. (It is about six inches narrower than the more well-known Hogan shoulder-width stance.)

[4] The supple golfer should adopt at the address a right foot pre-turned at 45 degrees and a left 90. The 45-degrees right foot holds the right side/leg sturdy to generate as much energy in the backswing as is possible with a short backswing; it is also better positioned to drive the lower body aggressively in the downswing. Thereby, it extracts as much of the potential energy available and transmits that into the dynamic rotational power in a golf swing.

The 90-degrees left foot encourages the downswing to pivot on the left heel and fan-slide the left sole *off the ground*; thus, the whole swing axis rotates 'effortlessly' on the left heel like a top spinning on its spindle.

These 45 and 90 degree orientations of the feet are key to distance. Jon Rahm has shown that a compact backswing does not limit the distance potential of a swing. What if Jon adopts the 45-degree right foot and the 90-degree left foot orientation? It can take him to greater distances.

[5] The driving distance has only increased 5 percent over the last two decades. https://www.pga.com/story/how-driving-distance-has-changed-over-the-past-40-years-on-the-pga-tour

[6] For shots less than a driver distance, a right leg revolving around the left leg on a limited follow-through momentum and still landing the right foot across the target line can be desirable as it can increase distance for fairway woods and mid to long irons without compromising accuracy.

To tap into the maximum distance potential of a driver tee shot, the rotational follow-through momentum can allow the lower body to rotate 360 degrees around the target line and land the right foot near its initial address position. Such a rotation of 270 to 360 degrees on follow-through allows the golfer to follow the ball in flight. Indeed, it is eminently possible for the golfer to track the flight of the ball when the follow-through is at the isosceles triangle position to the right arm reaching the midnight position.

[7] The Hogan Swing has a left foot turned 22 degrees, which effectively blocks the rotational movement in the downswing. The Iron Byron does not have a left leg to block its downswing; hence it was able to achieve the Convex Strike on the ball. YT Siew adopted a left foot pre-turned 90 degrees toward the target; this is as close to not having a left leg/foot at all! Hence, YT was able to emulate Iron Byron's Convex Strike.

EPILOGUE (1)

YT BECOMES THE FIRST GOLFER TO ACHIEVE THE CONVEX STRIKE

In the epilogue of my first book, *The Reflex Convex Swing*, I observed that Iron Byron, a club-testing machine, executed the Convex Strike on the ball.

The machine generated a convex bend shaft as it approached the ball, as can be observed in the video from the time segment 0:09–0:13, available here: https://youtu.be/-1Gr-vOA4sI (posted on August 11, 2014).

Scan QR code with your smartphone to watch Iron Byron executing the Convex Strike on the ball.

During this time segment, when Iron Byron's arm is in the 6:30 a.m. position, the shaft of the club exhibits a distinct convex bend. In the subsequent moment, with the arm in the 5:45 position and the clubhead approximately 6 inches from impacting the ball, the shaft retains its convex bend. After impact, as the machine's arm reaches the 5:30 position, the shaft transitions to a concave bend and maintains this shape throughout the rest of the follow-through.

Here is a speculation: the shaft may have impacted the ball with a slight convex bend or a straight shaft, then transitioned to a concave bend after impact. However, the YouTube instructor made no mention of the convex bend phenomenon as the shaft approached the ball. This fleeting moment could have been overlooked due to a lack of expectation or dismissed because no professional golfer has exhibited a convex bend shaft before striking the ball.

How could Iron Byron, a machine, execute a Convex Strike?

The primary reason is that *the machine lacks a left side or leg to block the downswing on the follow-through.* The momentum of the downswing remains unimpeded before the club strikes the ball, as the machine's only arm simply drags the club with the convex bend shaft through the ball.

The absence of a left leg or side to block the momentum of the rotational follow-through is a distinct advantage in achieving a Convex Strike.

How did amateur golfer YT Siew achieve it?

YT executed the Convex Strike by eliminating the 'blocking' influence of the left leg and foot during his follow-through swing.

In addition to developing the necessary strength in his left shoulder to generate potential energy in his backswing and the required rotational speed in his lower body during the downswing, YT made unique changes to the foot orientation of the Convex Swing System.

YT pre-turned his right foot 45 degrees and his left foot 90 degrees toward the target at the address. This positioning allowed for very efficient energy generation with a notably short backswing. At the top of his backswing, his left arm was in the 9 o'clock position, requiring only a 15-minute movement on the clock face to reach the ball in the 6 o'clock impact position.

The decision to use a very open left foot, pre-turned 90 degrees(1) toward the target, was a stroke of genius born out of necessity. YT aimed to ensure two things:

1. Direct shifting of body weight onto the left heel in the initial move of the downswing.

2. Unobstructed rotation of the lower body by the very open left foot and leg during the rotational follow-through of the downswing.

Transferring body weight onto the left heel allowed the swing axis to rotate on it, akin to a spinning top rotating on its spindle. It permitted the left leg or side to pivot on the left heel and fan-slide the sole off the ground. These actions[1] facilitated near-frictionless movement throughout the downswing, enhancing its rotational efficiency—essential for achieving the elusive Convex Strike on the ball.

Emphasizing the early transfer of body weight onto the left heel helped stretch the X-Factor, potentially allowing the shaft to retain a convex bend nearer to impact the ball.

By pushing the Convex Swing System to its limits, YT has made a significant contribution to the journey toward achieving the unprecedented feat of a Convex Strike[2] on the ball. YT is the first human to accomplish this.

A human golfer has replicated the achievement of Iron Byron, a club-testing machine. This validates the 'fleeting moment' of Iron Byron approaching and utilizing the convex bend shaft to strike the ball[3]—a feat long considered impossible.

YT has made history, and deservedly so.

His effort has removed the mental block that the Convex Strike is not humanly possible. It will encourage others to do so.

[1]The left foot pre-turned 90 degrees toward the target and the pivot fan-slide off the ground have the effect of not having a left leg/foot blocking the downswing much like the Iron Byron having no left leg at all.

[2] The straight shaft strike by YT can be considered as a Convex Strike due to the rolling shutter effect making the shaft appear less convex. But the shaft has not transitioned into a concave bend at any time throughout the impact zone.

[3] The Iron Byron has most likely done the 'pure' Convex Strike: that requires the shaft to have a distinctly convex bend shaft throughout the impact zone and perhaps, at impact on the ball. There is little doubt that any professional golfer with a sufficiently high rotational speed of the lower body driving his swing can do the 'pure' Convex Strike.

EPILOGUE (2)

⬦⬦⬦

THE CONVEX SWING IS EASY TO LEARN

The Ben Hogan Modern Swing has been established for more than a half-century and is ubiquitous. However, there are elements in the Hogan method that make it hard to play with; some of them even limit the swing's distance potential. The Reflex Convex Swing was devised to redress the shortcomings of the Hogan Swing.

The Main Differences between the Swing Concepts

The Hogan Swing and Convex Swing concepts differ in three areas:

1. Width of Stance

    The Hogan Swing uses a 'shoulder-width' stance.

    The Convex Swing uses an 'armpit-width' stance that is about 6 inches narrower.

2. Orientation of the Feet at the Address

    The Hogan Swing has the right foot set perpendicular (90 degrees) to the target line and the left foot turned toward the target at 22 degrees.

The Convex Swing has the right foot turned toward the target at 20–45 degrees and the left foot at 60–90 degrees. The higher degree of turn of the feet is more suitable for the supple golfer to tap into the distance-designed benefits of the swing. And they promote the anti-clockwise rotational movement of the lower body in the downswing.

3. Movement of the Lower Body as the Motive Force

The Hogan Swing uses a less efficient 'slide and turn' movement of the lower body over the wide 'shoulder-stance' to power the downswing. It also taps into the supination of the left arm and hand and the unfolding of the bent right arm to increase the power of a two-handed downswing.

The Convex Swing uses the rotational movement of the lower body over a narrow 'armpit-width' stance as the primary motive force to power the downswing, much like that prevalent in field sports. The dominant power of the lower body is transmitted through the stretched muscles of the core, the upper body, and the left arm to drag the club through the ball.

Key Differences and Advantages of the Convex Swing

The differences between the setup positions of stance and foot orientations at the address determine the dynamics of the movements of the backswing and downswing.

They determine the way the backswing generates the energy for the swing and the transmission of the energy generated to power the downswing.

They determine the type and efficiency of the movements used. And the degree of reflexiveness achieved in the swing.

Here are the key differences and advantages of the Convex Swing:

1. In the backswing, the right foot, pre-turned 20–45 degrees, determines the length of the backswing. The left shoulder pushes immediately against a very sturdy right side or hip. The left shoulder revolves less around the swing axis. The left arm arrives at the 10 o'clock top of the backswing position. The resulting short, compact backswing can be executed more reliably.

2. In the backswing, the left shoulder pushes immediately against the right side/hip. The maximum coil is attained with the left arm at the 10 o'clock top of the backswing position. The X-Factor of 60 degrees between the shoulder and hip planes occurs much earlier. Thus, the generation of energy in the short compact backswing is more efficient.

3. At the address, the positions of both feet are pre-turned toward the target, with the hip line left of the target line. This primes the first move in the downswing to occur more readily and shifts the body weight onto the left heel. The push off the ball of the right foot and the rotational thrust of the left side, hip, and leg plant the body weight onto the left heel; this stretches the X-Factor, thereby creating more energy for the downswing force.

4. The resultant rotational movement of the lower body revolves more easily around the narrow 'armpit-width' stance. The very open, pre-turned left foot facilitates the momentum of the rotational downswing via a pivot fan-slide

movement. They allow the left side to lead the dependent movement of the connected components of the downswing. That maintains the connectedness of the swing.

5. The rotational movement of the lower body is the prime motive force driving the downswing. The dominant power of the lower body is transmitted through the stretched muscles of the core, the upper body, and the left arm to drag the club through the ball. There is no need to tap into other sources of power. The focus is to build on the power of the rotational movement of the body.

6. The 'leading' movement of the lower body allows the left side to dominate the downswing. The dragging movement of the left shoulder and arm allows the clubhead and clubface to remain square to the swing path. There is no need for any conscious effort to square the clubface at impact. This takes the timing of the impact on the ball out of the swing, thereby allowing the downswing to be played reflexively.

7. The 'leading' movement of the left side ensures the components of the downswing stay connected. This dispenses with the need to sequence their respective movements. This frees the mind from the disruptive sequencing thoughts, resulting in a free-flowing swing.

The descriptive differences enumerated in the above sections suggest that the movements of the Hogan Swing are more complicated than those of the Convex Swing. This is especially true when executing the downswing.

In the Convex Swing, the focus is just on the rotational movement of the lower body, dragging the connected components and the club through the ball. This frees the mind of the disrupting thoughts of sequencing the movements of the swing and timing the impact on the ball. Thereby, the swing becomes more reflexive, consistent and easier to play with.

The Convex Swing is Simple to Learn

The static parts of the swing consist of the following:

1. At the address, assume a narrow 'armpit-width' stance with the golf ball position at the center of the stance.

2. At the address, pre-turn the right foot toward the target 20–45 degrees and the left foot 60–90 degrees.

The dynamic parts of the back and downswing consist of two conscious movements:

1. The push *solely* by the left shoulder in the backswing maintains 'connectedness' in the backswing to arrive at the desired CTC top of the backswing position. From there, the torsion felt in the muscles of the core and the tension felt in the stretched muscles of the right side/leg and left side/leg make it instinctive to start the downswing.

2. The push-off the *ball* of the right foot initiates the downswing and rotates the left hip or thigh to transfer the body weight onto the left heel. The continuous, unrestricted rotational movement of the lower body pivots on the left heel and fan-slides the sole of the left foot *off the ground* to take the swing to a rotational follow-through finish.

Before the swing starts, it is necessary to adopt a posture where the components of the body are suitably connected in their preset orientations to each other at the address. The posture at the address needs to display the static elements of the Convex Swing.

(Setup procedures for posture and stance, etc., are described in Chapters 4 and 6 of *The Reflex Convex Swing*.)

Then, the above-mentioned conscious dynamic 'leading' movements determine the subsequent dependent connected movements of the components of the back and downswing. The subconscious responses of the dependent connected movements to the two 'leading' movements make the Reflex Convex Swing truly reflexive.

When the push of the left shoulder is automatically done, the golfer gets into the desired CTC top of the backswing position.

As the backswing is completed, the stretched muscles of the right and left sides make it instinctive to trigger the start of the downswing.

The rotational movement of the lower body in the downswing primarily determines the outcome of the golf shot.

It allows the left side to dominate the downswing.

The leading left side, shoulder, and arm drag the club through the impact zone to the ball. Because the components of the swing are connected, they respond to the dragging movement of the 'leading' left side. This dispenses with the need to sequence the movement of the dependent connected components. The clubhead stays square on the swing path. This eliminates the timing of the impact on the ball from the swing.

Then, the mind is truly freed of swing thoughts that disrupt the free flow of a powerful swing.

A swing made with the big muscles of the body in both the backswing and the downswing is more consistent and less prone to succumbing to pressure.

A Single Focus on the Key Movement of the Backswing

Ultimately, pushing solely with the left shoulder in the backswing can become the only conscious movement of the Convex Swing.

When the backswing is done well, the stretched muscles of the right side at the CTC (Connected, Taut, Compact) top of the backswing make it instinctive to initiate the downswing. Thus, this focus on a single movement to start the backswing makes the Convex Swing easy to learn and play with.

It makes the Convex Swing truly reflexive, allowing a golfer to play in the zone more often.

A golfer gets into the zone of Zen golf more often.

[1] A detailed description of a setup procedure to establish a suitable posture and stance, connect the components of the body in their orientations preset at the address, and then execute the backswing can be found in Chapters 4 and 6 of *The Reflex Convex Swing*.

Figure 1.1 of Chapter 1 of this book displays the basic concepts of the Convex Swing.

[2] Since the push solely by the left shoulder to start the backswing is so important, it pays dividends to strengthen the 'pushing' muscles of the left shoulder. Drills 1 and 2 of Chapter 7 are described in detail in *The Reflex Convex Swing*.

When the left shoulder is suitably strengthened, the backswing can be executed by focusing on the left shoulder *solely* pushing the left arm and club on an inclined arc backward and upward till it reaches the top of the backswing. Figure 4.1 of Chapter 4 of this book shows that pushing is done solely with the left shoulder.

The checkpoints of a well-executed backswing culminating in the CTC top of the backswing are described in Chapter 4 of this book (Figure 4.2). A more detailed description of the backswing is available in Chapter 2, pages 30–39, of *The Reflex Convex Swing*, a DIY precursor to this book.

Note: This Epilogue is for those who have not read my first book, *The Reflex Convex Swing*, published in 2020. It summarizes the key points of the Convex Swing.

www.ingramcontent.com/pod-product-compliance
Lightning Source LLC
Chambersburg PA
CBHW020721160726
47993CB00006B/2291